# STRANGER IN A HOMELAND

## A Year in the Land of the Rising Sun

KYLE MCCORMICK

Cover design by 100Covers
Interior design by FormattedBooks

# Contents

# Foreword

This book started off as a one-size-fits-all informational guidebook about living abroad, along the lines of "A *Gaijin's* Guide to Japan." However, as I began writing, I realized that I had nothing new worth saying. There was no single nugget of wisdom that I could impart—no matter how wittily worded—that could not be found elsewhere a thousand times over, written more succinctly, and likely for free. As I continued to write about my first year in Japan, though, I realized something: I don't want to inform you. I want to *inspire* you.

Any discerning reader may now be asking, one eyebrow raised skeptically, "And just who are you? Why should I care about your life?" The answer is quite straightforward: Within the context of living abroad for an extended period, I'm nobody.

That's the point.

Before coming to Japan, my life was unremarkable. Like many American 20-somethings, I was staring down the barrel of a future that promised roughly two thousand 40-hour work weeks and then a short break before death, and I found myself dissatisfied. Never one to settle for a half-measure, I began researching alternatives. I stumbled upon a Japanese language school that was hiring native English speakers from abroad and applied immediately.

I had no particular advantage in pursuing this new life. I had never been to Japan before, couldn't speak the language beyond a handful of phrases half-remembered from childhood anime, and had no prior teaching experience of any kind. All that I did have was enough clothes to fill a suitcase, a high tolerance for failure, and a strong desire to get off my couch and do *something* with my life.

Anyone with half these qualifications can have an equally remarkable time. Whether you're a recent college grad looking to explore the world or a middle-aged divorcee on the brink of a mid-life crisis, a new life is now literally just a few clicks away. I chose Japan due to my longstanding interest in its culture and history, but I could have just as easily ended up hauling lumber in Alaska or trawling the Icelandic fjords—and so can you. Today, opportunity is a low-hanging fruit in near-limitless supply. All that you have to do is reach out and grab it.

Another point that I hope you'll take away from my story is this: The only way to truly understand another country or its people is to live there. Once you've immersed yourself in a culture, day after day, and it begins to lose to the mystical appeal that drew you toward it in the first place, you've only just begun. Don't get me wrong—vacations are rewarding in their own right. However, without any investment beyond whatever sum of money you've already resolved yourself to spend, there's no potential for lasting, meaningful change.

So, as you read my story, try to picture yourself in my shoes. Imagine what you would do with an abundance of free time in an unfamiliar land. Picture the adventures you could have and the wonderful, unique, considerate people you might meet.

Then, if you so choose, make that dream a reality.

This is important, so let me reiterate: You can move abroad. Not the generic "you" in the sense of my readers at large, and not at some vague, idealistic point in the future when the stars align, and opportunity arrives at your front door with a wink and a smile. You, reading these words, can do as I have done, and as millions worldwide are doing at this very moment.

From the moment I applied for my program to the day that I stepped off a plane some 6,500 miles from home, the entire process took only four months. Consider that, then make this the moment your adventure begins. There's a beautiful, brilliant world out there, and it's yours to explore.

Time to chase the horizon.

# Preparation

Now, just because I was resolute in my decision to move abroad doesn't mean I was without reservations. Aside from the obvious risk of soul-crushing isolation, any number of logistical issues can arise when making a life-change of this magnitude. Securing a visa, finding employment—anything can go wrong, and experience suggests that it usually does.

To that end, I can only credit good fortune for my apparent success. The company that hired me had been recruiting from abroad for nearly half a century and was well-accustomed to the process. They handled as much of the paperwork as possible, leaving for me only a few quick visits to the Japanese Consulate-General in Detroit.

In November, a little less than a month after my initial job interview, I was approved. With remarkably little effort or proof of competence on my part, I was authorized to live and work on the other side of the world. My company informed me that I would be sent to Nagoya, a city that lies approximately one-third of the distance between Kyoto and Tokyo.

A sense of bewilderment set in, then. Prior to receiving my visa, the plan had remained a bit of a fairy tale in my mind: a grand dream, certain to be dashed at any moment against the grim shores of reality as I snapped awake once more to my insipid life. Now, though, I began to feel a sense of cautious optimism. In my hands, I held a very official document certifying that I would indeed be starting a new life in three short months.

Not sure where to go from there, I began tying up the loose ends in my life: notifying my employer, allowing my apartment lease to lapse, and saying my goodbyes to friends and family. Fully half of them did not believe me at first when I told them my intention, but they all came around after seeing me charged with genuine excitement for the first time in my adult life.

The last few weeks of December flashed by in an unbroken string of bittersweet farewells. My entire family was in town for the holidays, giving us one last opportunity to spend time together before I left. Looking back, I scarcely remember what we did or said, but it was a better send-off than I ever could have asked for.

Then, quite suddenly, I was setting an early alarm on the eve of my departure. My bags were packed, and I was ready.

# The Journey Begins

I left for Japan on a cool winter's day in January, flying out of the affront to human decency that is Detroit Metro Airport. I woke up at the crack of dawn, left with my family, and said my goodbyes. Truthfully, the magnitude of what I was about to do had not yet fully set in. Even as I stepped onto the plane, my only thoughts were of what movies to watch.

The flight was eventful, exactly as no good flight should be. It was a straight 14-hour shot, and, in true Delta Airlines fashion, my seat's TV was stuck on the language-selection screen. I switched seats in what I thought to be a clever moment of aerial stealth, only for the flight attendant to pointedly announce that we were free to move around the cabin as we pleased. The second seat's TV began emitting a high-pitched whine within minutes of its intended use, which forced me further onward.

However, as they say, third seat's the charm. I found a functioning TV several rows behind my original seat and settled in for the flight. Twelve hours, half as many B-movies, and one unsatisfying nap later, we landed at Chubu Centrair International.

Customs was surprisingly straightforward, considering no one spoke more than a few words of English. The officers simply

*Mountains over Russia*

checked that my paperwork was in order, smiled politely, and waved me through the gates. On the other side, I met up with two other teachers-in-training, Kate and Sterling. We made our introductions and took a train to Nagoya proper. Once in the city, we dropped our bags off at the company's dormitories (where the three of us would be staying for the initial week of training) and set out into the night.

How to describe that first night in Japan? Well, simply put, it was over-whelmingly foreign. The city, the language, and the people, who moved en masse with the homogenous efficiency of a well-oiled machine, were—to borrow a phrase from Douglas Adams—almost, but not quite entirely unlike anything that I had ever experienced before.

Compared to my previous travels, Japan felt like a different world entirely. Three jet-lagged, bedraggled foreigners aimlessly wandering the streets of Nagoya garnered more than a few sideways glances, and I hadn't yet decided whether I was offended or flattered by this unwarranted attention.

Nagoya is Japan's fourth-largest city, with a population pushing 2.3 million. Located on the eastern seaboard of Honshū—Japan's main island—it is a primarily industrial city specializing in automotive mechanics. This is mainly due to the fact that Toyota City, the headquarters and namesake of the nation's biggest company, lies just shy of an hour from the city center.

All of this has resulted in a bustling downtown commercial district, filled with the sort of administration needed to support such an industry. However, as the three of us wandered through the streets of our new home, we scarcely noticed the many monolithic skyscrapers looming above. Instead, our focus was fixed solely on the spectacles around us.

Sterling, Kate, and I soon found ourselves near Nagoya Station and the iconic Mode Gakuen Spiral Tower at its southern entrance. Our stomachs began to quietly assert their interest in the dozens of restaurants near the station, from which drifted a tantalizing array of mouthwatering scents. After weighing our options, we settled on a curry restaurant with a picture menu and enjoyed

*Nana-chan: Nagoya Station's unofficial mascot*

a hot meal with an Asahi beer—a Japanese mainstay. We chatted while we ate and got to know each other a bit better.

Kate was an eccentric character who, by her own admission, was only in Japan to wait out what she considered to be the impending crash of the American housing market. She had no particular interest in Japan as a country, but she seemed excited to be living abroad.

Sterling, on the other hand, was a self-described weeaboo, or Japanese cultural fanatic. He had organized and chaired his high school anime club and had long dreamt of living in Japan. For all that, he displayed a certain level of disdain for the basic cultural mores of his new home. He openly drank on the streets, smoked outside of the designated areas, and seemed to revel in the (albeit ridiculous) gangland connotation of walking with his hands in his pockets. When I asked about this, he not-so-subtly implied that he hoped to find employment with the *yakuza,* or Japanese mafia, once he had learned to speak Japanese.

Thus ended that line of discussion, as far as I was concerned.

While my new friends were eager to continue exploring the city into the early hours of the morning, I began to realize just how exhausted I was shortly after dinner. Given my scattered hours of restless sleep on the plane, along with the overwhelming sensory onslaught of our new home, there was nothing that I wanted to do after leaving the restaurant so much as sleep. I returned to the company dormitories and fell, bone-tired, into bed. I still had no idea what to expect from the coming weeks, but I was glad to have found some new friends to experience them with.

The following day, the three of us were free to explore further, and we did so with gusto.

Our first order of business was to drop off an order for *inkan,* or red ink seals, which are required in lieu of a signature on most official documents. In doing so, we learned our first Japanese Survival Tip:

JPY 101: Nobody speaks English.

For seemingly no reason, barring my childhood obsession with English-language Japanese cartoons, I had been under the impression that Nagoya was a veritable paradise of multilingualism.

"But wait!" the astute reader might ask. "Wouldn't that go against the very nature of your job as an imported English teacher?"

Why, yes. It would.

We managed to order our seals at a nearby department store through the wonders of gesturing, broken English, and shattered Japanese. From there, following the advice of a great many online guides, we took the train to Atsuta Jingū. (Side note: If you've never stood in utter silence on a crowded platform while a dozen strangers openly stare at you, it's quite the experience.)

Atsuta is a sprawling, open-air shrine founded in the second century AD to house the *Ame-no-Murakumo-no-Tsurugi*, or Heavenly Sword of Gathering Clouds. Legend holds that the god of storms, Susanoo, gifted this sword to mortals after slaying an eight-headed serpent. As such, it remains one of the nation's three most sacred treasures, known as The Imperial Regalia of Japan.

Shintoism, Japan's indigenous religion, advocates the worship of *kami:* benevolent spirits that inhabit all things. For example, a forest has its own *kami*, as does each tree, river, insect, and animal within it. So, too, do smartphones, homes, cars, and people. Combined with a traditional mythological pantheon, there is no shortage of deities in whose name to build a shrine.

This particular shrine was dedicated to the eponymous Atsuta-no-Okami, alongside the Five Great Gods of Atsuta. Since its construction nearly two millennia ago, the shrine has enjoyed the financial and political support of some of Japan's most notable historical figures, including Oda Nobunaga, Toyotomi Hideyoshi, and the Tokugawa *shogunate*. (The *shogunate* was a hereditary military dictatorship whose power rivaled that of even the emperor for several centuries.)

The shrine grounds were packed that day due to the ongoing *Hatsu-Ebisu* New Year's festival. Food stalls lined the entranceway on either side, offering everything from chocolate-covered bananas to fried octopus skewers. It was a very old-meets-new affair, with somber, enrobed monks ordering deep-fried ice cream puffs from flashy street vendors. Even with hundreds of people milling about, there was an air of quiet deference that you rarely encounter in the States. People walked around each other unobtrusively, spoke in hushed whispers, and every single person bowed in reverence to the *torii* gates as they left.

It's easy to forget sometimes, due to the abundance of cutting-edge technology, that Japan is *old*. Properly old. And for all that time, its history has been preserved incredibly well. Atsuta, for instance, is ostensibly just three wooden huts and a dirt path spread throughout a forest, but it has been meticulously maintained for millennia. When the shrine was first constructed, around 100 AD, Japan was a loose collective of Iron Age tribes warring over a scarcity of resources. Yet this unassuming little shrine has survived the thousands of tumultuous years since. By comparison, when the Statue of Liberty turned green after 34 years, America just shrugged and adjusted the color on its postage stamps.

Before leaving the shrine, I made a brief pit stop at the main office to purchase a *goshuinchō*. As proof of devotion through pilgrimage, this small, blank book serves as a sort of passport to the afterlife. Most temples and shrines have a unique *goshuin*, or red seal, which they apply to a blank page in a visitor's book for a nominal fee—typically ¥300. (Of course, by the time a collector fills their first 80-page book, this fee begins to seem much less nominal.) A monk then writes a personalized message in traditional calligraphy denoting the location and date, plus a short blessing. In theory, the more *goshuin* a worshiper has, the more pious they must be.

From the shrine, we planned to continue onward to Nagoya Castle, which also rested comfortably near the top of all of Nagoya's "must-see" lists. It could be reached from Atsuta via either the subway or a long walk through the city's residential districts—we opted for the latter, mainly because we did not yet feel comfortable braving the Japanese metro.

About seventy minutes into the hour-long walk, I began to suspect that we might be lost. Ten minutes later, my suspicions began to deepen, and fifteen more minutes of fruitless wandering all but confirmed it. This would become a recurring theme of my time in Japan: Regardless of the destination, I routinely arrived ten to twenty minutes later than expected.

Thank goodness punctuality isn't a fundamental pillar of Japanese society.

The castle was impressive and, as one of my brothers would later remark, strikingly reminiscent of those in our childhood strategy games. Sterling, Kate, and I were unable to enter because of renovations, so we explored the castle grounds for a bit before beginning the walk back to our company's headquarters. The three of us stopped at a McDonald's on the way home in accordance with the adage, "When in Rome, do as you've always done."

Much of the next week was consumed by work, with training from noon to 9:00 PM every day. While nothing of great interest occurred, I did learn a few more valuable lessons during my lunch breaks:

JPY 101:

- Convenience stores are a foreigner's best friend. There's one on every corner, and they carry everything from nudie mags to children's toys.
- Toilets have heated seats and more buttons than a three-piece suit. The bidets function on a "randomly and liberally" basis.

# Early Days

Once my initial work training was over, I moved from the company dormitories into my own apartment. This luxurious 208 ft² studio was located in Ōzone (pronounced Oh-zoh-nay), in Kita Ward. For the metrically-inclined, that's approximately 19.3 m²; alas, not quite as spacious as a one-car garage.

While the size (or lack thereof) did take some getting used to, it provided a few distinct benefits:

- I could vacuum the entire apartment without moving my feet
- There were only three surfaces physically capable of collecting dust
- I was always within arm's reach of the TV remote

The apartment itself may have been unimpressive, but it was conveniently located next to Ōzone Station. This was representative of Ōzone as a whole, in fact—not terribly exciting in its own right, but remarkably convenient. And although it may have held a slight edge in that regard, it was by no means unique.

Urban Japan is a place unlike any other in its pursuit of gratuitous convenience. Within easy walking distance of my apartment, there were three competing *conbini* (convenience stores), two shopping streets, and well over a dozen vending machines. Several months after I moved in, one of the convenience stores was replaced by a JoyJoy karaoke parlor, as the chain deemed their existing establishment, ten minutes away on foot, too distant.

Speaking of which, it quickly became apparent that Japan's interest in vending machines went far beyond mere accessibility. The half-dozen or so that were immediately visible from my front door were, more or less, par for the course in their abundance. Any given city block might have had as many as three machines on each corner, plus a few scattered along each street for good measure. This obsession was not restricted to cities, either. Some of the more remote vending machines that I would eventually discover included in the backwater hills of the Kiso River Valley, atop Mt. Fuji, and in the delightfully rural fishing village of Obama. (Although this village was established several hundred years before the birth of America's 44th president, they still charmingly elected to adopt him as their de facto mascot shortly after his inauguration. In doing so, they requisitioned perhaps the world's only Obama-themed vending machine.)

These machines contained the typical assortment of coffee and tea that one might expect, plus some more peculiar offerings: cans of bean soup, video game cartridges, contraceptives, and the like. Along one lonely stretch of road in Tokushima Prefecture, intrepid explorers could even find an innocuous little machine selling home-cooked packets of curry and rice prepared that very morning by a kindly local grandfather. Or, in the case of one particular machine across the street from my apartment, bottles of *dashi*—an umami-rich fish stock integral to Japanese cuisine. These bottles generously included a pickled fish carcass, encased within, to ensure adequate rancidity at the time of purchase.

After moving into my new apartment, I spent much of the following week exploring my neighborhood, trying to get my bearings among the tightly packed mid-rises. During one such stroll, having been lured into a nearby restaurant by the enticing fragrance of simmering beef, I learned an important corollary to my first Japanese Survival Tip:

JPY 101: Nobody speaks English. English-speaking restaurants, in particular, *do not speak English.*

Upon entering, I was met with a wave of blistering heat and a chorus of "*Hai, irreshai!*" (Welcome!) from the staff. They seemed, I thought, unreasonably surprised when I requested a table for one person, even going so far as to ask whether I had instead meant two, or three perhaps. Looking around myself in confusion, I confirmed that I was indeed alone. I was subsequently seated at an uncomfortably large table with a series of inlaid grills.

At that time, I was incapable of reading any Japanese beyond the scope of my own name; therefore, I found the pictureless menu terribly confusing. However, I noticed with some relief that it offered "Bilingual support, on request!" I flagged down a waitress and gestured toward the offer. She gave a terse nod of understanding and wandered off, returning sometime later with an older, distinctly monolingual gentleman.

He began to read me the menu—in Japanese—pausing every so often to gauge my understanding. Somehow unable to sense my confusion, he continued reading until the menu was finished.

And I'll be damned if it didn't help. From his exaggerated gestures, I was able to glean that this was a *yakiniku* restaurant, which meant that it served all-you-can-eat raw meat en masse to be cooked by the party at each table. And let me emphasize the word "party," here, because the staff's initial confusion at my solitude suddenly made sense. Every item on the menu was a heaping pile of raw meat which, when cooked, could comfortably feed four to five people. I was barely hungry, and, truthfully, already worn out by this unexpectedly complicated encounter. Still, having requested a translator, I felt committed to ordering something. I selected at random, and the gentleman returned to the kitchen with a satisfied smile.

So it was that I ended up with a pile of pork quite nearly the size of the original beast, plus a bottle of sake that I had hastily tacked on in the hope of chemically dulling my embarrassment. The meat was quite tender, and, after choking down the first few blackened crisps, I got into the rhythm of eating one piece while simultaneously cooking the next. After half an hour, though, I had barely made a dent in it.

Once it became clear that I was doomed to fail, I flagged down a server and requested the check. I planned to collect the bill, then nurse my remaining sake and injured pride at the table. Unfortunately, as I couldn't communicate this intention to the server, he retrieved my bill and walked over to the cash register. He then stood there, casting expectant glances in my direction. (I would later come to understand that this is the norm at many Japanese restaurants—your bill is handled directly at the register by the staff.) Resigned, I left a pile of raw meat and two-thirds of my sake at the table to pay, then beat a hasty retreat. I returned home that night utterly defeated, full to bursting, and not half as drunk as I would have liked.

This still ranks among my ten fondest memories of the year. Had I been intimidated by the language barrier, or each individual set-back along the road to eventual embarrassment, that night would have been like any other: utterly forgettable. Instead, it became a memorable experience that paved the way for hundreds of equally confusing culinary excursions to come.

My other early lessons in the ways of Japanese culture were far less dramatic and came over the course of the next several weeks. For instance, while wandering around the city, I came to appreciate the many ways that Nagoya had found to consolidate its rich cultural history with its modern identity.

In the case of religion, Japanese civilization has simply grown up and around traditional places of worship. It's not uncommon to find Shinto shrines in the middle of a busy thoroughfare or tucked away behind an apartment complex. Similarly, strip malls and the like are often sprawled haphazardly around Buddhist temples. (For the sake of clarity, temples are Buddhist, and shrines are Shinto. The distinction is purely semantic.)

Occasionally, old and new feed off of and support one another. Osū Kannon, Nagoya's preeminent Buddhist temple, is one such example. The temple was built in 1333 in present-day Hashima, Gifu Prefecture. It was moved to Nagoya in 1612 to coincide with the construction of Nagoya Castle, as well as escape the repeated flooding that it had endured in Gifu. A modest market district began to develop around the temple, bringing increased patronage to both.

The district has modernized in the many centuries since its humble beginnings—it now contains two covered shopping streets, dozens of restaurants, and several hookah bars—but still retains its traditional feel, thanks to the feudal-era temple at its heart. This attracts tourists and locals alike, who, in turn, support the temple with their offerings.

Other cultural revelations were notably more surprising. Truthfully, the sheer absurdity of many Japanese stereotypes had led me to believe that I would arrive to find them vastly overblown. And, while that proved true for the most part, certain aspects of Japanese culture were simply, undeniably foreign to me.

One example is interpersonal dynamics, which are governed by a rigid hierarchy of age, company position, and social status. Strangers establish this relationship within minutes of meeting, which often results in shows of self-aggrandizing called "mounting." This is where men use the three B's—bribery, bullying, and bullshit—to vie for the top position. (As an aside, in researching this topic, I made the mistake of Googling "Japanese men mounting." This was inadvisable, to say the least.)

"But wait!" you may be thinking. "Every culture has some form of social hierarchy!"

That's true. But in Japan, it dictates the flow of conversations, as well as the very words that speakers choose to use.

Generally speaking, Japanese has two tiers of spoken deference: *keigo* (polite) and *tamego* (casual). Within *keigo,* there are at least two more varieties: one to humble yourself and one to uplift others. The words also tend to be longer, which is considered more polite.

Another stereotype about Japan that proved true is the nation's wholehearted obsession with Pokémon. From the election of honorary prefectural ambassadors to Yokohama's annual Pikachu Outbreak festival, Japan is simply saturated in pocket-sized paraphernalia. My next tip, then, should come as no surprise.

> JPY 101: Every man, woman, and child in the nation plays Pokémon Go.

I know I've never been one to shy away from a good hyperbole, but this one may actually be true. I played the game religiously when I first arrived in Japan, having discovered in it a way to live out my childhood fantasies while simultaneously exploring my new home. Several times a week, I would walk from my apartment to a nearby raid (the game's in-person cooperative event) to find men and women of all ages huddled together, eagerly awaiting the chance to catch a rare Pokémon.

And when I say, "all ages," I mean *all* ages. While young men made up the bulk of the players, elderly women getting some exercise were a close second. Next came excitable children with their parents in tow, then a handful of office workers. The least represented demographic among my fellow players was—to my vast disappointment and minimal surprise—young women.

Once a month, the game would hold a special event called Community Day, which further encouraged players to go outside and interact with each other. On one such occasion, I took the train to Tsuruma Koen, a large park near my apartment that was sure to have at least a few players scattered around.

Or, as it turned out, a few thousand. On the way there, I'd noticed that the train was a bit more crowded than usual, but I had figured that everyone must have been on their way to a festival downtown. Never in my wildest dreams had I imagined I would arrive at Tsurama to find it filled to the brim with aspiring trainers—no mean feat for an open-air park—but I did.

All around me, groups of players roved haphazardly about, somehow managing to avoid collisions even with their faces glued to their screens. And, to the event's credit, it was a more social affair than the game's usual gatherings. People congratulated each other on their victories and talked excitedly about their recent catches. At one raid within the park, featuring Mewtwo (a perennial fan favorite), players gathered in such numbers that those who had finished battling were unable to continue onward until the players around them—still tapping furiously at their screens—had dispersed.

# Settling In

**B**efore moving to Japan, I had done a fair bit of research into the problems that one might reasonably expect to encounter when moving abroad. Most of the advice was straightforward: The language barrier, dietary restrictions, and social isolation seemed to be the repeat offenders. However, I fancied myself above the day-to-day struggles of those who had come before me and—in what hindsight suggests was nothing more than arrogant naiveté—disregarded most of this advice.

But when I got settled into my new life, I realized *why* everyone has the same advice.

Let's start with the language barrier, for instance. I mentioned earlier the fact that nobody spoke English (hence my job), so I'd quickly learned to rely on the miracle of modern translation technology.

Except, Japanese is a tricky language, with no fewer than three written components. The first and most complicated of these, *kanji*, is logographic Chinese, appropriated in the fifth century AD and modified in the centuries since. While there are only 2,136 *jōyō kanji* (those that are commonly used in day-to-day life), there are upwards of 85,000 characters in total. Most of these have multiple pronunciations, as well as any number of written stylizations, creating a functionally infinite number of variations.

*A typical example of* kanji: rei, *meaning "zero." As in, the
odds of me ever mastering* kanji *are precisely* 零.

The second script, *katakana*, is used for *gairaigo*, or loan words from other languages—primarily English and Portuguese. However, due to the intricacies of spoken Japanese, many of these loan words have been modified beyond recognition.

You see, all consonants in Japanese must be accompanied by a vowel, with the exception of ん—a nasal sonorant that takes the place of both "n" and "m." As a result, any foreign word adopted into the Japanese lexicon must first be assigned vowels for each lone consonant, often to baffling effect. For example, many of my students loved to post pictures of their food on *i-n-su-ta-gu-ra-mu* (Instagram). Similarly, anyone walking beneath the iconic Golden Arches might soon find themselves inside a *Ma-ku-do-na-ru-do* (McDonald's). Other words maintain their general structure but are truncated for the sake of brevity, such as *a-pa-to* (apartment) or *pa-so-ko-n* (personal computer).

The third script, *hiragana*, is a strictly phonetic alphabet derived from the original cursive script of Chinese calligraphy. It is used in conjunction with *kanji* to augment and modify their meaning. *Hiragana* can also be placed above each *kanji* to provide the phonetic equivalent for anyone incapable of reading them outright—namely, children and foreigners.

Of course, when combining these three distinct syllabaries into one cohesive sentence, there's bound to be room for error. Even the most advanced translation software occasionally drops the ball, offering results that are, at best, comically inaccurate. At worst, they can be dangerously misleading.

According to Google Translate, for instance, my toilet offered options such as "ass" and "video," neither of which sounded very appealing in its own right. When read together, however, these characters combined to form "big tits."

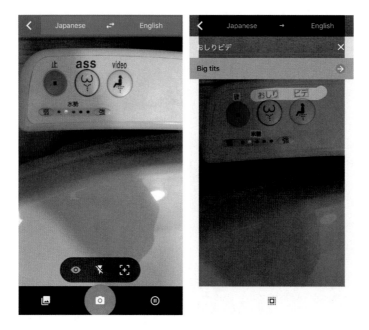

It truly is a mysterious and beautiful language.

Another tip that I had casually disregarded was that Japanese people are gentler than Americans in their actions and words. What people neglected to mention was that this has resulted in an entire country built for light touches and slight frames, neither of which I possess.

I've never been known for my refinement of motion, but I was utterly graceless by Japanese standards. Maybe it's because much of the country's infrastructure was built when the average man was 5'2" (157 cm), but I found myself constantly slamming open doors and bumping into walls.

As if being the tallest, whitest person in any given situation didn't garner enough attention, I'd now added "lumbering" to my list of adjectives. If there was ever a stereotype about Americans being brutish and uncoordinated, I have not done us any favors abroad.

# Motsunabe

In early February, one of my adult students, Koji, invited me out for drinks and *motsunabe*: Japanese hot pot. On the way to the restaurant, he informed me that *motsu* means "offal"—a dish that, in my limited experience, is well-deserving of a certain adjectival homophone.

A fellow teacher named Saori and I met up with Koji after work one preposterously windy evening. The three of us made our way to the restaurant huddled within our coats, buffeted by icy gusts on all sides. By the time we arrived at the restaurant, clothes disheveled and chilled to the bone, I was ready for a drink. Thankfully, Koji (a businessman of some renown) was more than happy to accommodate me. From our conversations in class, I had already gathered that he was a somewhat prolific drinker, but I had not yet come to appreciate the true extent of Japanese drinking culture.

You see, most Japanese salarymen are perilously overworked. It is not uncommon to work 12-hour shifts, five days a week, plus the occasional weekend or holiday. Even then, it's considered quite rude to leave the office before your superiors. As a result, once your own tasks are complete, you may have to kill time for several hours to maintain the pretense of working. Understandably, this has resulted in a workforce that is in dire need of some stress relief.

And alcohol has long been Japan's relaxant of choice. As early as the third century, Chinese historians felt compelled to record their island neighbors' debaucherous ways —Chengzuo, one of the Jin dynasty's most prominent historians, remarked in his *Records of the Three Kingdoms* that even Japanese funerals were remarkably convivial.

*Sake* (distilled rice wine) was the historical spirit of choice due to the relative ubiquity of its primary ingredients—rice and water. These days, however, beer rules supreme. Walking through Nagoya's club district on a Saturday night, one is sure to espy hordes of diurnally respectable businessmen roving the streets in search of cheap booze and frisky women, plus a few laid out along the curb for good measure. In their hands (and on their breath), the hoppy remnants of an Asahi Super Dry can be found.

So it was that Koji knew just what to recommend for my first drink, then my second, and then my third. Soon, the warmth of the spirits had soaked into our bones, and the three of us were able to converse without the chatter of teeth. It became apparent that Saori and Koji were well-accustomed to each other's company and often went out drinking together. They regaled me with stories of their past adventures, occasionally touching on topics that spoke of a bond deeper than that of a student and a teacher.

Koji made the usual set of inquiries that I had grown accustomed to answering. ("Where are you from? Oh, Michigan! I've heard it's nice there this time of year. Oh, it's downright miserable? Hmm. Well, how do you like Japan?") He wasn't just being polite either; most of my students took a genuine interest in my hometown. Although it may not always appear to be the case due to the nation's isolationist policies, many Japanese people are fervently interested in American culture.

I, in turn, asked about his life and family. Koji informed me that he had two daughters around my age, the youngest of whom was a model. He brought up several pictures of her on his phone.

"Isn't she beautiful?" He asked, beaming proudly. She was. I half expected him to offer to introduce us, as several of my other middle-aged students had done. Alas, he did not.

The conversation soon turned to interests, and from there to music. Koji asked if I played any instruments, and I confessed that I did not. I asked him the same, and he informed me that he plays the piano. Or used to play, rather; he had learned piano when his eldest daughter was in grade school so that he could help her practice for recitals. Now that she had grown up and moved to Canada, he no longer found the time to play as often. Still, he did on occasion to remind him of simpler times. It was, on the whole, unbearably endearing.

The *motsunabe* arrived half an hour later, and it looked heavenly. The pot was still boiling as it was set at our table, and the *motsu* was barely recognizable as such. It was surprisingly delicious, as were the many sides that came with it: raw horse, fried chicken, and *dango*—balls of mochi on a bamboo skewer. (Mochi, for the uninitiated, is a rice byproduct without any discernible state of matter. It is a gelatinous solid, produced entirely through rigorous beating and the suspension of disbelief.)

We ate, drank, and spoke with the carefree exuberance of friends in the making. The night passed pleasantly. Too soon, we rose to pay our check—more successfully, I might add, than during my ill-fated excursion at the *yakiniku* joint. Fancy that.

As we were leaving the restaurant, Koji invited me to the first baseball game of the upcoming season. He had a season pass with the Chunichi Dragons—Nagoya's home team—and very much wanted to show an American how the Japanese played baseball. I had also mentioned that my home team was the Detroit Tigers, who had been well past their prime since I was in grade school, so he may have simply wanted to redeem the sport in my eyes.

I accepted his generous offer, and we parted ways. When I next taught his class, our conversations were those of newfound friends.

# Illuminations

Later in the month, I traveled with another co-worker, Jenna, and two of her friends—Akari and Koichi—to the Winter Illumination in Nabana no Sato: an immense botanical garden thirty minutes south of the city. Illuminations are Japan's response to the fact that seasons exist and the effect that winter has on its eternal quest for lasting beauty.

From spring through autumn, visitors can enjoy all manner of flowering life within the garden. In February, however, its scenery is markedly less... well, scenic. Even in Japan's relatively temperate climate, what little foliage remains is sparse and grey—exactly as whelming as one might expect of a garden in winter.

Japan is a truly scenic land, blessed with crystalline lakes and soaring mountains. Unfortunately, this has resulted in a severe lack of arable land. In 2016, just shy of 11.5% of its total landmass was suitable for agriculture, with a further 0.5% becoming unusable per year. Therefore, it has had to economize its floral beauty into convenient pockets of green. When even these spaces prove incapable of bearing fruit, they simply string a few quintillion flower-shaped lights and call it a day.

Thus, Illuminations were born.

On the way to the garden, I was alarmed to discover that Koichi's car had a TV installed on the dashboard. Not just the enhanced navigation system/smartphone accessory that has become commonplace in America, either; this was a full-on, Saturday-morning-cartoon TV, positioned such that it never left his line of sight. Japanese traffic laws already closely resemble entropy, so the inclusion of this additional distraction was quite unnerving. Thankfully, Koichi was the diligent sort, and the four of us made it to the garden in one piece.

Nabana no Sato was remarkable. Its sheer size alone led me to believe that it would be worth a return trip during the off-season, once the Illumination had ended and nature had reclaimed its rightful place. As it stood, however, the great fields of multi-colored lights made for a beautiful stroll. The four of us wandered through the softly glowing labyrinth for what felt like hours before arriving at that year's feature display: an animated light show of Mt Fuji, depicting its mythology and history.

Following the light show, we stopped at a small outdoor food court near the entrance to pick up some *karaage*—lightly-breaded, marinated fried chicken: a modern Japanese staple. Once we had finished eating, the four of us returned home to Nagoya.

Shortly after that trip, I came to realize that Illuminations are not the only way that Japan compensates for its lack of greenery. Another trick is to simply reappropriate common outdoor phrases to include the subterranean. Nagoya's Central Park, for instance, is neither central nor a park; rather, it is a vast, underground shopping center. Similarly, Ōzone "Garden" is anything but.

*Not quite Eden*

# Ise Jingū

In late March, my friends Trevor, Audrey, and I traveled to Ise Jingū, the Grand Shrine in Mie Prefecture. We had arranged the trip several weeks prior, to the extent of "Hey, let's go to Ise!" and did no additional research whatsoever. Thankfully, I have done a great deal since.

Ise is dedicated to Amaterasu, the Shinto sun goddess and pantheon matriarch. As such, it is widely regarded as one of the most venerable sites in Japan. According to one of the oldest classical books on Japanese history, *The Nihon Shoki*, the shrine was established in the year 4 BC by the princess Yamatohime-no-mitoko (thereby narrowly defeating Christianity in the religious war of firsts). The princess was ordered by her father to travel the land in search of a suitable place to enshrine Amaterasu's sacred mirror, the *Yata no Kagami*. Alongside the sword at Atsuta, this mirror is one of Japan's Imperial Regalia.

The princess wandered the land for approximately twenty years before heeding the call of the goddess (or that of her weary feet) in Ise. She posted fifty bells around the nearby Uji-tachi fishing village, declaring it to be the domain of the goddess, and it has remained hers ever since.

Of course, fifty bells and a small fishing village do not a grand shrine make. Over the next several centuries, additional shrine complexes were erected in Amaterasu's honor, expanding her territory to a size roughly that of central Paris.

Trevor, Audrey, and I agreed to meet at Nagoya Station around 10:00 AM, planning to establish a route to the shrine from there. In doing so, we discovered that Ise is comprised of two main shrines—not to mention another

123 lesser shrines—about five kilometers apart: Gekū and Naikū. What scant reading we had done suggested Gekū as the place to begin our adventure, so we booked three tickets on a southbound train.

After a suspiciously cheap train ride, which took nowhere near the anticipated two hours, our train reached its final stop at Tsu Station. We disembarked and consulted our phones for assistance.

Audrey deduced that we were still about ninety minutes from Gekū, but we had no idea how to purchase another ticket to Ise. The three of us wandered around the station for some time before tracking down a ticket machine, only to discover that it was out of order. I'm glad I had friends with me, because I'm certain that's exactly when I would have given up and returned to Nagoya if I had been alone.

Trevor, whose Japanese was leagues better than mine, managed to convey our frustration to a station employee, who insisted that the ticket machine was fully functional. Because this was Japan, and everyone but us knew everything, it had miraculously repaired itself by the time we returned.

If Japanese public transport is a well-oiled machine, my friends and I were the rusty, misshapen cogs determined to make it fail. We picked up our tickets and hopped on an express train that would take us the rest of the way there.

We arrived at Gekū an hour later to discover a quiet, secluded assortment of shrines in the middle of the forest. While many Buddhist temples strive for opulent grandeur, Shinto shrines tend to favor quiet demurity—and Gekū was no exception. With a modest main shrine and a series of random forest paths leading to a dozen or so unassuming smaller structures, it wasn't much to look at. But, when we were actually there, in the midst of the forest, its natural serenity made it easy to fall into a sort of trance. People wandered around slowly, nodding amiably as they passed one another.

Visiting Gekū also led me to realize how much I had missed even the barest semblance of nature in Nagoya. Even though the shrine was essentially just a small patch of forest surrounded by city, it was bliss to walk on spongey earth for once rather than unyielding concrete.

*The forest of Gekū, in all of its arboreal splendor*

On our way out of Gekū, I stopped at the monks' office to purchase a second stamp for my *goshuinchō*. Curious about what I was doing, Audrey wandered over.

"What's that?" she asked, seeing me pull the little green book out of my backpack.

"It's a *goshuinchō*," I explained, opening it up to show her my stamp from Atsuta Jingū. "You can use them to keep track of the temples and shrines that you've visited."

Her eyes lit up at this. She bit her lip, then ventured, "How much does it cost?"

Thus, she purchased her own, and we each added a stamp to our collections.

After Gekū, we began a pilgrimage of sorts toward Naikū. Of course, being unable to find the traditional walking path between the two shrines, this meant that we walked along a busy road for an hour. That was the first week of spring, however, and the countryside was in rare form. The sun was shining, birds were singing, and the faint aroma of budding flowers drifted pleasantly on the warm breeze. After two months of winter-deadened senses, it was beyond bliss.

As we walked toward Naikū, the three of us encountered a small side-street littered with shrines. While it wasn't explicitly closed off, the unmanned stalls and exposed overhead wiring led us to believe they weren't expecting visitors. This allowed for some uninterrupted sightseeing—a rarity, in Japan—and some quiet time near a small lake.

One of the little joys of exploring Japan is running into these hidden pockets of traditionalism when you least expect it. Many of them were relegated to their own forgotten corners of the countryside in the rapid modernization of the last few decades, but they're still out there, waiting to be discovered.

Immediately before Naikū, we reached Oharaimachi Street, a historical district dedicated to the shrine. This provided an opportunity to experience the shrine as it had been centuries past, and, of equal importance, a chance to eat.

While I had visited other historical districts before, Oharaimachi was the first that was downright crowded. Thousands of people strolled along the main street and its many offshoots, enjoying the shops and the weather. *This* is what I had hoped to find in a shrine: a chance to experience tradition, rather than staring at it from behind the guardrail of a museum.

The street was lined with dozens of shops and restaurants, selling everything from fried chicken shish kebabs to obsidian statuettes. After a quick walkthrough of the district to assess our options, we settled for a mishmash of fried shrimp skewers, candied honey fries, and *tamagoyaki*—which I can only describe as "egg loaf."

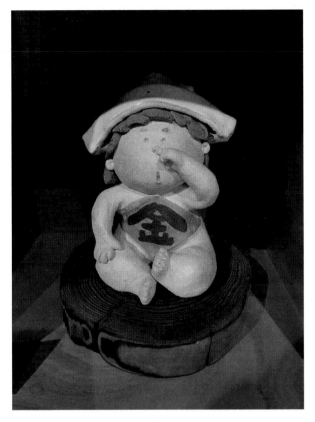

*I have never in my life been so tempted to spend $80*

Once we had eaten our fill (and then some), we continued onward. After a brief, misguided jaunt halfway up the neighboring mountain courtesy of Google Maps, we finally arrived at Naikū.

If Gekū was but a patch of green in the middle of a city, Naikū was a forest in truth. Beyond a short entranceway, the path grew less cultivated, lined on both sides by towering Japanese redwoods. These ancient conifers have grown massive in their centuries of uncontested dominance, reaching a size to rival that of their Californian cousins.

*My partners in crime, getting in touch with nature*

From the entranceway of Naikū, a wooded path led deeper into the forest. A half-dozen *torii* gates lined the path, and every visitor bowed at each. Even though Naikū is more popular than Gekū, the fact that it's spread over a much wider area helped it feel significantly less so. While we must have passed a hundred or so people within the quiet confines of the forest, it never felt crowded.

Like Gekū, Naikū adheres to the *Yuitsu-shinmei-zukuri* style of architecture, which is characterized by extreme austerity. Along with Gekū and the adjoining Uji Bridge, Naikū is rebuilt every twenty years in accordance with Shinto beliefs on the ephemeral nature of existence. While replacing a few featureless huts in the woods every couple of decades doesn't sound like too costly an endeavor, remember for a moment that Ise covers an area roughly the size of central Paris. This, along with the exacting specifications to which each rebuild must adhere, makes it quite the undertaking.

Due to the sheer scale of this event—known as the *Shikinen Sengū*—the shrines rely on extensive community involvement in the form of several preparatory events and festivals. The year 2013 marked Ise's 62nd rebuild, and, while I can't comment on the previous 61 iterations, I have to imagine it's worth the effort. The constant renewal to ancient standards has resulted in a spectacle that's both millennia-old and decades-new, much like Japan itself.

Aramatsuri-no-Miya *is a satellite shrine within the forest dedicated to Amaterasu's vibrant spirit*

Finally, the three of us made our way to the main shrine to pay our respects. Having already made offerings at several dozen others throughout the day, we were getting short on funds, so we agreed to make this our last. Audrey and I made a quick detour to pick up Naikū's stamp, then the three of us made our way to the exit.

We left Naikū, reluctantly, at sunset. By the time we finally got back to Nagoya that night, we had been traveling for a solid twelve hours. We ate a quick dinner together, then parted ways.

In the end, it made for an immensely satisfying trip. Rarely have I found a single day so fulfilling or so enjoyed resting my feet afterward. My only regret was that we were unable to see any of Ise's famed wild chickens, which are traditionally believed to be Amaterasu's divine messengers. While this must be difficult given their inability to speak, it's a considerably better vocation than "McNugget."

# Inuyama Fire Float Festival

In early April, I took day trip with Trevor to the Inuyama Float Festival. This festival has been held in Inuyama City more or less annually since 1635, when the lord of Inuyama Castle at the time requested an event to honor Haritsuna Shrine and the *chinjugami*—local guardian deity—enshrined within.

The festival coincides with *hanami*, or cherry blossom viewing season, which is something of an unofficial holiday in Japan. Locals and tourists take to the streets in droves during this two-week period, flocking to the parks and neighborhoods where the flowering trees are most abundant. Although *hanami* only lasts for around ten days, with the prime viewing making up only a third of that time, this period accounts for upwards of $6 billion in tourist revenue every year.

(So enamored are the Japanese with *hanami* that, as I edit this book during the COVID-19 pandemic one year later, people are still attending viewing parties en masse despite the government's direst warnings.)

While there are hundreds of *hanami* festivals in Aichi Prefecture, Inuyama's is widely recognized as one of the most remarkable. People travel from all across southern Honshu to witness the spectacular parade that takes place every year in the old town streets near Inuyama Castle.

The festivities began with a dozen or so floats, practically brimming with occupants, gathering in the courtyard at the base of the castle's embankment. While they prepared for the day to the lilting backdrop of flute music and *taiko* drums, street vendors began to hawk their delectable wares.

To say that I'd grown unaccustomed to hunger in Japan would be an egregious understatement. To say that I'd spent three months in a gluttonous stupor would be closer to the truth, and that beautiful spring day was no exception. One of the true joys of Japanese festivals is the sheer volume and variety of food available: *okonomiyaki, takoyaki,* chocolate-covered bananas—just thinking about it makes me salivate like a dingo in a nursery. That was also one of the first pleasantly warm days of the year, which, alongside a total lack of responsibilities, made for perfect day-drinking conditions. Trevor and I picked up some beer and a pile of fried chicken, which we enjoyed as we wandered up the hillside toward the castle.

Unlike Nagoya Castle, which was reconstructed in the late 1950s, Inuyama Castle has endured the passage of time largely unscathed. Originally built in 1440, it is often thought to be the oldest surviving castle in Japan—although poor record-keeping makes this difficult to verify. Whether or not it is strictly the oldest, however, Inuyama is certainly one of only 12 castles to have remained unreconstructed since the end of the Edo Period (1603-1868).

The castle has seen no fewer than 26 different rulers in the last six centuries, with the final dozen hailing from the Naruse Clan. Research suggests that they relinquished control after running out of names beginning with "Masa."

- Naruse Clan

    1. Naruse Masanari (1617–1625)
    2. Naruse Masatora (1625–1659)
    3. Naruse Masachika (1659–1703)
    4. Naruse Masayuki (1703–1732)
    5. Naruse Masamoto (1732–1768)
    6. Naruse Masanori (1768–1809)
    7. Naruse Masanaga (1809–1838)
    8. Naruse Masazumi (1838–1857)
    9. Naruse Masamitsu (1857–1869, 1895–1903)
    10. Naruse Masao (1903–1949)
    11. Naruse Masakatsu (1949–1973)
    12. Naruse Masatoshi (1973–2004)

We waited in line to enter the castle for some time, but it was simply too long, and our restless feet demanded we return to the festival grounds. After finishing our chicken and beer, we restocked on both and made our way toward the banks of the nearby Kiso River. Along the way, we ran into another teacher and her friend from out of town. Together, the four of us walked to the river.

The Kiso River originates in the foothills of Mount Hachimori and flows through approximately 140 miles of southern Honshu before emptying into Ise Bay, near Nagoya. The portion that runs through Inuyama is lined on both sides with dozens of cherry trees, whose blossoms illuminate the area like beacons of vernal genesis. We took our time ambling lazily in their shade, enjoying the riverside breeze.

Eventually, however, the setting sun forced us back to the relative warmth of the festival grounds. The main event was scheduled to begin shortly after sunset, and we had no intention of missing it. By the time we made it back to the castle's base, people had already begun congregating in the streets.

As we waited, the ominous thrum of a *taiko* drumbeat began, far off in the distance. It drew ever closer, accompanied by the sound of something immensely heavy grinding on the pavement. Soon, we were able to see the source of this commotion: a series of towering wooden floats, covered in lit paper lanterns, blazing a trail through the cool night air.

Festivalgoers scrambled out of the way as the floats spread throughout the streets of Inuyama, propelled by dozens of shirtless men. As one approached the corner where we were standing, it skidded to a halt with a dangerous forward lurch. The float, which had fixed wheels and no means of turning, had to find another way to make it around the sharp bend.

Trevor and I watched in awe as the dozen men who had been pushing the contraption positioned themselves beneath beams that jutted out from each corner and *lifted* the float—burning lanterns and child inhabitants included— off of the ground. They then spun, with alarming rapidity, turning under the juddering tower's immense weight.

While one might reasonably be nervous in the immediate vicinity of a whirling wooden tower adorned in flames, it's important to remember that Japan is an incredibly precise country. The maneuver had clearly been well-practiced and was carried out without a hitch.

After the float had trundled past, the crowd around us began to disperse. Trevor and I had long since passed the euphoric stage of day drinking and found ourselves exhausted, so we made our way toward the station. We returned to Nagoya once more, satisfied at having seen and done both everything we could and nothing of importance.

In the end, the Inuyama Float Festival was not the largest festival that I would attend in Japan, nor even the most magnificent. However, my memories of that day—drifting aimlessly beneath the swaying cherry blossoms and standing in awe before a towering spire of flame—are ones that I will cherish forever.

# An aside

**A**t the end of March, my co-workers, Jenna and Saori, set out for greener pastures. Jenna returned home to England to enroll in grad school, and Saori moved closer to her new husband's workplace. In their place came Felicity and Fumika.

Felicity was a New Yorker, fresh out of college, who had come to Japan with her childhood friend. She was a few years younger than me, but a fun person and a hard worker.

Fumika, on the other hand, was an absolute rock star (and, full disclosure, my current long-term girlfriend). She came from a small town on the northern coast and had never met a single foreigner before entering high school. However, she'd always had a fondness for Latin music, so she majored in Spanish in college. Seeking to experience more than her small corner of the world—a sentiment which I viscerally understood—she found a program that let her study abroad in Mexico for one year. By her recollection, she was perhaps the only Japanese native in the entire country.

In Mexico, Fumika only spoke Spanish. However, she realized that she would need to speak English to travel to non-Hispanic countries, so she began to teach herself after returning to Japan. Fumika learned the entire English language in a little over a year using nothing but the internet and her television. She then got a job as an English teacher and, after a couple of years, was transferred to my school. From there, the rest is history unfolding.

Whereas Jenna and I had been agreeable workplace acquaintances, Felicity, Fumika, and I would soon become fast friends. They'll show up here and there throughout my story, so they're good names to remember.

# Golden Week

On April 30, 2019, Emperor Akihito relinquished his title and authority to his son, Naruhito. This was the first time since 1817 that an incumbent Japanese emperor had voluntarily abdicated, and it caused quite a stir.

You see, while the emperor no longer holds any formal authority, he is by no means powerless. Traditionally, Japan is a deeply hierarchical society, with the emperor wielding absolute control.

After World War II, then-emperor Hirohito was forced to concede this power to the newly-instated parliament, in accordance with the post-war constitution. He was allowed to retain his title, however, and continue serving as "the symbol of the State and of the unity of the People."

As this decidedly vague provision suggests, the emperor's reign continues to influence policy in many ways. As the emperor changes, so too does the Japanese era, which forms the basis of Japan's official date/time system. The emperor is also traditionally held to be a direct descendant of the Amaterasu (the Shinto creator goddess) and, thus, the mortal figurehead of the country's indigenous religion.

A few small changes have already occurred, as of writing this, but the lasting effects of this nigh-unprecedented abdication have yet to be seen. So, what did this change mean to me, as someone with neither a strong connection to the Shinto faith nor a vested interest in Japanese policymaking?

It added two extra days to my already lengthy spring vacation, Golden Week.

Golden Week is a glorious period in late April, when the entire overworked population of Japan takes a much-needed break to recuperate from the last several months of incessant productivity. It was also my first meaningful stretch of vacation since my arrival, which allowed me to spend time with two highly anticipated visitors: my parents.

They flew in a few days before my vacation officially began. I made my way downtown as quickly as possible after work and met them outside of their hotel in Sakae - Nagoya's premier nightlife district. We had a lovely reunion in the raucous streets, but the previous three months had passed by in such a blur that it felt as if only a moment had passed since I'd seen them last.

Once our reunion was complete, my dad mentioned that they hadn't gotten the chance to eat yet. Weeks earlier, I had mentioned a rather peculiar chain restaurant called Ichiran Ramen, where you never see nor speak to the wait staff or the other patrons. This piqued their interest, so we made our way over.

Ichiran consists of a series of enclosed single-person booths, arranged in a line. It serves *tonkotsu* (pork broth) ramen: a perennial favorite of Sakae's many drunken revelers. Patrons place their orders at a large ticket machine in the restaurant's entranceway, which requires blessedly little in the way of spoken Japanese. My parents and I collected our tickets—my father and I opting for a beer as well—and sat down at our booths. Thankfully, at that particular Ichiran, it was possible to fold back the walls of our booths so we could speak to each other.

We had ordered our ramen at the ticket machine, but now we had to make choices as to the specifics: wide or thin noodles, spicy or mild, etc. These choices were listed in full on a sheet of paper that awaited us at our booths, simply needing to be circled.

Unfortunately, they were listed in Japanese. Even after several months, my spoken Japanese remained pitifully insufficient, and it would be more apt to say that I could identify sounds rather than read. So, we settled for my usual technique in situations such as those: circling randomly. After a few short moments, a waiter came by—only his torso visible through a small window in the front of our booths—and appraised our selections.

He popped into view for a brief moment, unimpressed by the results of our haphazard ordering, and noticed that we were distinctly foreign. He returned moments later with English menus, mumbled a quick apology, and retreated from view.

After our ramen came, the wait staff closed the windows, and we were left to enjoy our food in peace—that is, except for my poor father, whose long legs clearly hadn't been considered in the construction of our cramped booths. Even in a splayed-out position that yogis might endearingly dub "The Gynecologists' Chair," he slipped off of the rounded stool a half-dozen times throughout the meal.

Once we'd finished eating, I walked my parents back to their hotel. They were visibly exhausted, and I had to work the following day.

⚯

The next morning, my parents met me bright and early in Ōzone. They wanted to accompany me to Seto, the small country town where I taught, to get a feel for how I spent a typical day. The commute from Ōzone to Seto took about thirty minutes by local train, passing through all manner of residential and commercial districts. The scenery became progressively more rural the farther we traveled, until we left the city in truth.

"Doesn't this all just seem so foreign to you, Kyle?" my mom asked as we passed a series of tightly-packed houses. Laundry fluttered carefree in the wind on every balcony.

"Not really," I replied after a moment's consideration. "This is just my regular commute now."

Truthfully, by that point, many aspects of living in Japan that had first seemed so novel and exciting had already become routine. As I saw the wonder and excitement written so plainly across my parents' faces, however, I began to feel that same spark rekindling within me once more.

We arrived in Seto shortly thereafter.

Seto is a peaceful town, set into rolling foothills well beyond the range of Nagoya's metropolitan energy. It is one of the nation's primary ceramic producers, a distinction that it has held for nearly 800 years. In fact, as the oldest of the six *Nihon Rokkoyo*—ancient Japanese kiln cities—Seto is often considered the birthplace of Japanese pottery.

The city's affinity for ceramics can be traced back to the 13th century AD, when an esteemed potter, Toshiro Kato, traveled to China to learn the secrets of Chinese porcelain. He resolved to bring this art back to his home country and, upon returning to Japan, discovered a source of clay in Seto that was unlike any other. Toshiro established his workshop there and began to teach what he had learned to the locals.

In the centuries afterward, Seto gained further acclaim for the glossy appearance of its glazed pottery. As tea ceremonies grew in popularity amongst the nobility, so did the demand for Seto's bowls and utensils. In 1804, a potter named Tamikichi Kato set out to hone his skills in Kyushu, which had the most advanced techniques at the time. Just as Toshiro Kato had done, he returned to Seto with what he had learned, and the industry modernized rapidly.

Today, ceramics remains Seto's main industry, as evidenced by the various artworks that can be found adorning walls and bridges within the city. There are still dozens of family-run pottery shops and kilns, but these days, Seto has expanded into the production of industrial ceramics.

Either way, the reputation remains. In fact, Seto is so strongly associated with pottery that a common term for ceramics throughout Japan is *setomono*, or "Seto ware."

I showed my parents around the shops that were closest to the station, as well as the local shrines that I frequented during my lunchtime wanderings. Fukagawa Shrine, a scenic five-minute walk from my school, is believed to be nearly 1,200 years old and boasts a pair of *komainu*—guardian dog statues—created by Toshiro Kato himself. Kamagami Shrine, farther up the northern hillside, features a unique kiln-shaped design and houses the spirit of Tamikichi Kato.

After I had finished our short tour, I went into work, and my parents returned to Sakae with an abundance of free time and a long list of my recommendations. So, while they were off gallivanting around the countryside, I stared wistfully at the clear skies through my classroom's window.

## The Eternal City

After two uneventful days, the three of us agreed to meet at Nagoya Station and take the bullet train to Kyoto. The station was exponentially more crowded than usual, but for Golden Week, they had pulled out all the stops. Multilingual attendants were posted every dozen feet, ready to assist travelers in the most efficient manner possible.

My parents and I had planned to rendezvous at a large golden clock near the station's main entrance, which I was having trouble locating. I approached one of the stationmasters, who sported an armband that read "English," and asked how to get to the station's main entrance.

He gave me a brief glance, then replied, "Mother?" As I was indeed looking for my mother, I simply nodded. He led me directly to where my father stood on the other side of the crowded station and asked, "Father?" I nodded once more, dumbfounded.

Japan's customer service (and readiness to baselessly stereotype) never ceases to amaze me.

The bullet train ride went by as quickly as one might expect, and we soon arrived in Kyoto. The first item on our docket was a walking tour that purportedly covered all of Kyoto's most photogenic sites. Rather than lugging our bags around the entire time, we decided to find a locker at the station in which to store them.

Unfortunately, several thousand other people had had the same idea, and available lockers were few and far between. We spent thirty precious minutes frantically searching through banks of lockers, casting sideways glances at the other poor souls doing the same, before finally turning to the limitless knowledge of the internet. A quick Google search revealed a secret storeroom beneath the station that could be located with relative ease, so we did just that, dropped off our belongings, and went outside to meet our tour group.

There, we met our guide, a young man named Go. He spoke fluent English, having lived in California for several years. Unfortunately, he had also picked up something of the Californian work ethic, which made him a stupendously mediocre guide. His idea of a walking tour was to raise one limp-wristed hand over his head as he wove his way through the teeming masses, turning back every few minutes to count how many people had fallen behind.

Still, he knew where to find the sights worth seeing. We started by visiting three lesser temples of the Rinzai sect: a branch of Zen Buddhism that believes enlightenment can be achieved through strict discipline, devout meditation, and the occasional beating.

One remarkable thing about Go was that, although he had presumably given this tour dozens of times before, he knew almost nothing about any of the sites that we visited. Indeed, he was alarmingly uncertain as to even the basic differences between Buddhism and Shintoism, an overarching theme of the tour. He went as far as to claim that "Shintoism is about life, while Buddhism is about death"—an assertion that did not sit well with the Buddhist practitioner in our group.

Still, he shared a great deal of information, and even though a conservative 40% of it seemed to be fabricated on the spot, we found it interesting, nonetheless. After the Rinzai temples, we made our way to Fushimi Inari, a 1,300-year-old shrine known for its thousands of vermillion *torii* gates.

The shrine sits at the base of Inari Mountain and enshrines Inari Ōkami, the patron spirit of rice, sake, and tea, as well as agriculture and industry. As these wide-ranging provisions form the economic and cultural backbone of Japanese society, it's understandably well-beloved. Fushimi Inari attracts millions of visitors each year, with over 2 million paying homage during the New Year's holiday alone.

The *torii* gates outline a 2.5-mile trail winding up the mountain, which takes several hours to walk on a good day. However, this Golden Week had attracted an absurd number of visitors, every one of whom stopped frequently for photographs. We were only able to go a third of the way before Go called it quits and led us back down the mountain.

Finally, the tour brought us to the Gion district in Kyoto proper, which is the last remnant of Kyoto's once-bustling Geisha industry. We wandered through the district, past tea houses and boarding schools, and learned about the decline of Geisha culture in modern Japan.

As we neared the end of the tour, my mother discreetly asked Go about the rumored connection between Japanese Geisha and prostitution. With an indignant huff, he pulled the whole group aside and—rather indiscreetly—announced, "She has just asked whether Geisha are prostitutes. This is an offensive notion that needs to be dispelled immediately. Geisha is a noble profession that is deeply rooted in Japanese history, and it's ignorant to imply otherwise."

Then he tacked on, almost as an afterthought, "Of course, these are beautiful young women serving wealthy men. I'm sure that some of them choose to have sex in exchange for certain favors or benefits."

That's... prostitution. What you're referring to is prostitution.

After the tour, we stopped by a restaurant in Pontochō, a riverside alley famous for its many bars and restaurants, before finally catching a taxi to our hotel.

As it turned out, our hotel was an attraction in and of itself. The trip there took us farther and farther from civilization, along winding forest roads and through sleepy country hamlets. By the time we reached our hotel, even our taxi driver commented that she was scared to return to the city alone.

Our *ryokan* (traditional Japanese hotel) was a secluded villa nestled at the base of Takao Mountain. We were welcomed at the door by several friendly workers, who relieved us of our bags and shoes. They provided us with child-sized slippers, which fit comfortably on my mother and uncomfortably on me. They simply did not fit my father. The proprietress, a spritely old woman with twinkling eyes and an easygoing smile, found this endlessly amusing and spent much of the next few days openly laughing at the size of my father's feet. My father was less amused by this, as he spent those days stumbling over the comically oversized slippers that he had been provided in their stead.

We had a traditional room, complete with conjoining futons. (In Japan, a futon is essentially a bedroll.) The room also came equipped with *yukatas*—a type of traditional Japanese wear that closely resembles a decorative bathrobe. We immediately changed into these and cracked open a much-needed beer from the mini-fridge.

*My wonderful parents*

The next morning, my father and I went out to explore the area around our hotel. This included a brisk walk along Kiyotaki River, a crystal mountain stream cutting through the valley's forest.

In the city, it's easy to forget that wilderness exists. The greenery that you see is carefully cultivated and in short supply, and that eventually becomes your image of nature. However, when you finally get back to a proper forest, with mountains and rivers, it's a very welcome shock to the system. Clean air, the earthy smells of dirt and chlorophyll—there will never be a suitable replacement for untouched nature.

*Here there be spirits*

During our exploration, my father and I encountered a young Asian couple who were coming back from a hike. We were considering going down the same trail from which they had just emerged, so I asked them in my best Japanese where it led. They looked hesitant, in a way that implied that my best Japanese wasn't good enough, and shook their heads. Then, to our surprise, the man responded in English, "Sorry, no Japanese." I figured that they must have come from a neighboring Asian country and left it at that, but as they walked away, my father chanced, "But English is okay?"

They turned around, clearly relieved, and with nary a trace of an accent replied, "Of course!" They then told us in great detail about the path ahead and went on their merry way.

For all that I occasionally disparage Japan for its outdated views regarding stereotyping, it's important to remember that it's often done without malice.

After a traditional Japanese breakfast, my parents and I returned to the city. There, we met up with our second tour guide, a tall South African woman named Lianca. ("It's like Bianca, but with an L," she offered helpfully.) Thankfully, Lianca was infinitely more knowledgeable than Go had been and was not afraid to bully her way through a crowd. More than once, we caught her reprimanding locals for walking against the flow of traffic, much to their indignant surprise.

The first stop of her bicycle tour was Rokuonji, commonly called Kinkakuji—the Golden Pavilion. You are allowed exactly one guess as to how it earned this moniker.

Formerly the retirement villa of shogun Ashikaga Yoshimitsu, Kinkakuji was converted into a Zen Buddhist temple upon his death. It's unique among temples in that it has burned down no less than three times since its initial construction in 1397. The first two incidents occurred during the Ōnin War of 1467-1477. The third was much more recent—1950, to be exact, when a pyromaniacal monk with severe mental illnesses razed it to the ground as part of an elaborate suicide attempt. Each time it was subsequently rebuilt using wood—a material widely known for its flammability—including the most recent reconstruction in 1955. But, honestly, what's the worst that can happen?

Oh. Right.

We visited many other Buddhist temples and Zen gardens during the tour, as well as a professional bonsai tree cultivator. While the Zen gardens were certainly impressive, some of the symbolism went a bit over my head. ("Doesn't that rock look like a sleeping cow? No? Okay, stand here. Tilt your head slightly to the left, then forward 30 degrees. Squint a bit, and... still no? I guess you just aren't enlightened enough, then, huh?")

Near the end of the tour, Lianca pointed out a statue of a portly, raccoon-like creature with seemingly misshapen feet. She introduced it as the tanuki, a mischievous canine native to Japan whose enchanted testicles supposedly allow it to accomplish extraordinary feats.

According to Japanese legend, the tanuki's glorious gonads grant it abilities such as shapeshifting, flight, and vocal mimicry. On top of that, their versatile vela are quite simply a traveler's dream. Throughout Japanese folklore, there are countless tales of tanuki using their abundant scrotums to carry heavy objects, ferry passengers across rivers, and shelter themselves from storms. If it weren't for the constant torture that they must endure from eternally stumbling over their own genitalia, I might find myself envious.

*How else does one catch birds?*                    *...I'll just swim, thanks.*

Following the discovery of the magically endowed woodland critters that would soon become my new obsession, we wrapped up Lianca's tour with a speedy bike ride through the backstreets of Kyoto. As we were returning our bikes to the rental shop, my mom commented on the lack of public trash cans. Lianca explained.

JPY 101: There are no public trash cans in Japan.

In 1995, members of the Aum Shinrikyo doomsday cult released punctured bags of sarin gas on the Tokyo Subway. This noxious chemical killed 13 people and injured thousands more, in what would become the worst terrorist incident in modern Japanese history. As public fear over subsequent attacks arose, the government decided that trash cans were too convenient a place for hiding chemical weapons, so they banned them. All of them. And people actually complied.

While this is obviously a sad story, it does speak volumes about the Japanese spirit. When something threatens the health or safety of others, everyone bands together to ensure that it can no longer do so—no matter the lengths required.

After the tour, my parents and I returned to our *ryokan*. It was still quite early in the afternoon, so we decided to visit one of the three nearby temples, Jingoji. There were scant few minutes left until it closed, however, and we happened to be several hundred feet below it at the base of Takao Mountain. This led to a brisk, drizzly jog up a slippery series of mossy stone steps, making it to the top out of breath and very nearly out of time.

Jingoji was, without a doubt, the single most spectacular temple that my parents and I visited in Kyoto. Established in the year 824, the temple consists of a series of rustic wooden structures spread along a plateau near the mountain's peak. As with many ancient temples, Jingoji features the unique *kumiki* style of joinery.

You see, Japan is a land of near-constant seismic activity. Despite making up less than 0.3% of Earth's landmass, the island accounts for nearly 20% of all high-magnitude earthquakes. In such an environment, rigidly constructed buildings would soon collapse under the pressure of the relentless vibrations. However, since the Heian Period (794-1185 AD), Japanese architects have utilized an ingenious system of interlocking wooden joints, called *kumiki*, in the construction of their buildings. This allows a structure to sway during an earthquake, redirecting the majority of the force. In fact, many ancient Japanese buildings have no nails or mortar whatsoever and are held together solely by the manner in which the building weighs upon itself at these joints.

Only Jingoji's treasure room was accessible at that time of year, but it alone contained 17 national treasures and 2,833 cultural artifacts. The head monk was more than happy to explain the significance of these in faltering English, displaying the same patient benevolence that we had been met with so often on our trip.

Before we left, the priest mentioned that the temple would be even more spectacular when the leaves changed color in early October, situated as it was atop a singularly verdant mountain. This would plant the seed for no less than three return trips during the year.

*Jingoji's treasure room*

That night ended the Kyoto chapter of our trip. The colorful temples, friendly locals, and clean mountain air made for an absolutely unforgettable experience. After a disturbingly tentacular breakfast the following morning, we hopped on a bullet train bound for Tokyo.

# The Big Mikan

My parents and I had hoped to catch a glimpse of Mt. Fuji from the window of our train, but the overcast that had plagued us for days continued to obscure our view. We spent much of the two-hour ride napping, lulled to sleep by the bullet train's gentle swaying. Considering it travels in excess of 200 miles per hour (320 km/h), this stability is nothing short of a miracle of modern engineering. If not for the scenery outside, whipping past faster than our minds could process, it would have been hard to tell that we were moving at all.

That is, until it came time to use the bathroom. For all that I had enjoyed the cloud-like embrace of my seat, all bets were off once I was crammed into the compact commode with my pants around my ankles. Suddenly, I became acutely aware that we were rocketing through the countryside at a speed that was quickly approaching "ludicrous," and that the slightest jostle could send me pitching forward to disastrous effect. However, through careful use of the "tripod" pose—feet spread shoulder-width apart, leaning forward with my non-dominant hand pressed firmly against the far wall—I was able to relieve myself with relative ease.

Moving on, then.

We arrived in Tokyo shortly thereafter. After some initial misfortune in navigating the Tokyo metro, we arrived at our B&B near the Roppongi nightlife district. The owner had left strict instructions on how to enter and maintain the apartment. These were a far cry from the cordiality that we had been met with theretofore on our trip, so we began referring to her as "Brunhild the Beast" amongst ourselves. Although none of us had met her personally, the threatening nature of her messages gave us the overall impression that she would be an unwelcome sight in an alley at night.

Once we had dropped our bags off at her astonishingly large apartment (taking great care not to scuff, bump, or jostle anything), we continued onward to Shibuya Crossing. This 9-way intersection is thought to handle up to 2,500 pedestrians at a time, and is emblematic of Tokyo as a whole (i.e., crowded).

Afterward, we stopped at a nearby *yakitori* place for dinner. The host took one look at us, made a few quick assumptions, and immediately sequestered us to the "foreigner corner." (Not to be confused with the poor, similarly-entitled sod who handles the ex-pat autopsies.)

This little alcove was akin to Harry Potter's childhood bedroom, but without all of the legroom. We decided to quickly peruse the menu before finding a more spacious restaurant, which was a critical mistake. Our empty stomachs won out against our cramping legs, and we settled in to order.

The night ended up being quite enjoyable. The food was wonderful, the waiter spoke English, and we discovered that we were able to stretch our legs to nearly three-quarter length by sacrificing our dignity. (I'm beginning to sense a pattern, here!)

When sleep finally came that night, it found us with full stomachs and smiling faces.

The next morning, we took the metro to Sensōji Temple's outer gate, *Kaminarimon*. Unfortunately, we had weather befitting the Gate of Thunder and spent much of the afternoon huddled beneath our umbrellas.

The gate stands tall on the outskirts of the temple grounds, next to Asakusa Station. Though it was originally built near Komagata in 941, it has been relocated and rebuilt various times throughout history. Along with statues of Fūjin and Raijin, ancient gods of wind and thunder, it supposedly protects the shrine from evildoers.

From the gate, the flow of the crowd led us to an old town shopping street called Nakamise. Most of the shops sold the typical assortment of touristy goods that one might expect: boxes of chocolate, plastic swords, children's masks, etc. However, a select few stores sold more unique items, such as be-spoke kimonos and hand-carved kabuki masks.

My father had heard tell of one such store in the district that sold high-quality knives. As a cooking enthusiast, he was intrigued. As an eating enthusiast, I was doubly so. After a bit of searching, we tracked down a small metalwork shop that fit the bill.

Unfortunately, the shop was outrageous. It carried an exorbitantly expensive array of knives, tools, and swords, none of which were feasible for purchase or portage back to the US. Chief among these absurdities was a $30,000 multi-tool, which was worth literally more than its weight in gold. (Trust me, I did the math.)

After declining to spend a year's wages on some glorified cutlery, we continued through Nakamise to the temple itself.

Sensōji is the oldest temple in Tokyo and is considered by many to be its most magnificent. Its history can be traced back to 628 AD, when two fishermen named Hamanari and Takenari unexpectedly found a golden Buddha statue entangled in their net. As it wasn't the least bit edible, they cast it back into the river and continued to fish. However, they found that each time they drew in their net, it contained only the statue.

In fear of the fatal impoverishment that could strike so quickly in pre-Feudal Japan, they collected the statue once more and took it to the village elder. Being a pious man (or a sly opportunist), he immediately recognized it as the bodhisattva of compassion, Avalokiteśvara. The elder joined the priesthood and converted his home into a reliquary to house the statue.

It continued to gain popularity and fame throughout the years, as many locals who prayed to the Buddha for prosperity found their wishes granted. Hearing tales of such miracles, an esteemed priest named Shokai Shonin visited the temple in 645 AD. He converted the elder's home into a proper temple, which was then named Sensōji. Upon doing so, he decided that the statue was too radiant to be seen by the unwashed masses. It has remained conspicuously hidden ever since.

Sensōji was ravaged by earthquakes and fire several times throughout the ensuing millennia, as ancient buildings so often were. The main building was most recently rebuilt in 1958, having been incinerated during an Allied air raid on March 10, 1945. Along with Meiji Shrine, it's the most visited spiritual site in the world, attracting over 30 million visitors annually.

For dinner, having decided to forgo our usual three hours of unproductive wandering, my parents and I elected to make a reservation at a *yakitori* restaurant in Roppongi. By the time we arrived, they had already prepared our table, complete with a personalized welcome note. Due to my trademark carelessness, it was quickly reduced to the crumpled mess seen below.

The following day we went to Ueno Park, a great sprawling place in the middle of Tokyo. We had no set plans other than to "experience the city," which, combined with a profound lack of English signboards, left us wandering aimlessly within the park.

However, my mother is never one to be discouraged by the threat of embarrassment. She took it upon herself to communicate our lack of intentions to the locals and, after several minutes of wild gesticulation, received tentative directions for a zoo and a temple. Bless her heart; the woman gets results.

Unfortunately, the zoo was inaccessible due to the crowds. We stopped briefly at the temple to pick up another stamp for my collection, then continued onward.

Our second stop of the morning was Meiji Jingū. This grand shrine houses the spirits of Japan's first modern monarchs, Emperor Meiji and Empress Shoken. As such, it has held particular significance for all other emperors since its construction in the 1920s. Since this Golden Week also celebrated Naruhito's ascension to the Chrysanthemum Throne, it was one of the most popular sites in Japan.

Much like Ise Jingū, Meiji lies within a peaceful forest in the middle of the city. The forest contains roughly 120,000 evergreens, from 365 different species, which were donated when the shrine was first built. Meiji is one of the younger Jingū—shrines with a strong connection to the royal family—but it feels as if it's been there since time immemorial. The shrine buildings are spread throughout the forest along a series of wooded paths, ultimately leading to the inner sanctuary.

Like any self-respecting shrine, Meiji boasts an extensive collection of sake barrels gathered from around the country. However, Meiji is unique in that it also possesses a respectable collection of wine—a spirit that Emperor Meiji had grown quite fond of during the westernization of his reign. While these are technically offerings to the gods, one must imagine that the donors don't mind having their logos emblazoned across casks in one of the world's most visited religious sites. Neither, I'm sure, do the monks mind the rate at which the barrels are replaced—as one jaded local commented, "The gods may drink it with their eyes, but the monks drink it with a smile."

Later in the afternoon, we took a taxi to the Pokémon Center Mega Tokyo—a building whose mere existence would have had my younger self veritably foaming at the mouth in excitement. My older self fared little better.

The store was full to bursting with plush figurines, playing cards, and keychains. It contained the exact breakdown of young children and nostalgic adults that I would have expected, and every single one of them looked ecstatic to be there. I left with several souvenirs to send back home with my parents and the vague sense that I had accomplished a previously undefined lifelong goal.

We reluctantly returned to Nagoya the next morning. I was finally able to see Mt. Fuji in all of its glory on the ride back, which redoubled my dedication to one day standing on its peak.

One of the last things that my parents had wanted to try in Japan was pachinko—a bewildering game that has somehow managed to flourish in direct opposition of Japan's strict anti-gambling laws. We returned to Sakae, tracked down a parlor, and entered.

Imagine, if you will, a maelstrom of sound. Overpowering, relentless, and coming from seemingly every direction at once. In the center of this deafening vortex, there is not the calm that one might expect, but rather enough flashing lights to make a blind man seize.

That's the basic premise of pachinko: overwhelming sensory stimulation.

Each pachinko machine is roughly the size of an ATM. The game centers around marble-sized metal balls, which are summoned by the turn of a dial. The balls fall, bouncing randomly off of protruding spikes, while the machine alternatively blares rock music and flashes anime breasts. We put my poor mother in the hot seat, leaving her to bear the brunt of the chaos.

After several minutes, the machine began to emit an even louder, panicked sound, along with some frantic Japanese instructions. My mother, unable to determine the cause of the machine's distress, simply sat there laughing uncontrollably, tears streaming from her eyes. An exasperated employee soon appeared and showed her how to make the alarm stop, much to the relief of our fellow patrons. We had no further trouble, but the employee wisely chose to supervise the remainder of our pachinko experience.

Thus, we managed to convert $10 into five minutes of bewildering entertainment—and two lollipops, received as a consolation prize in lieu of any actual money.

From there, all that was left was to grab a quick lunch and return my parents to their hotel to prepare for their pre-dawn departure the following morning. We picked a nearby Hawaiian-themed pancake house that one of my students had recommended and set off on foot. En route to the restaurant, we began to hear the upbeat pulse of pop music echoing through the busy streets from afar, accompanied by a great deal of enthusiastic yelling.

"What do you suppose that is?" my dad asked, clearly intrigued.

"Hmm, I'm not really sure," I replied. "Want to check it out?"

With little else on our schedules, the three of us simply exchanged glances, shrugged, and set a new course.

As we made our way over, we noticed another group directly in front of us heading in the same direction: five young girls, dressed in flowery skirts with low-cut tops, practically skipping with youthful exuberance. I began to have an inkling of what we were walking into.

Three streets over from the main thoroughfare, my suspicions were confirmed. We found a small, pop-up idol concert—or, in more pessimistic terms, fifty middle-aged men drooling over four young women.

Idols—young girls who have fought their way into the spotlight through appearance or talent and whose subsequent growth is recorded and marketed to the public in its entirety—have become a mainstay of Japanese pop culture in recent years. While there are certainly some darker aspects to idol culture (for reference, 25 is generally considered the age at which an idol is no longer marketable to the public), most fans are simply well-meaning individuals who seek a sense of vicarious achievement. In following the growth and success of this young woman (or, rarely, man) fans can relive their own lost youth without any of the risks.

The three of us watched the concert for a while, then continued on our way toward the pancake house. After eating the most decadent pancakes to ever grace the face of the earth, my parents returned to their hotel. The next morning, they flew home to America.

As my first visitors in Japan, my parents' stay had been indescribably rewarding and refreshing. Being able to show the people I love around the new life that I had built was a joy unlike any other, and one that I would seek to replicate as often as possible throughout my remaining stay.

# Oktoberfest

**C**ome July, I could feel the festival bug stirring within me once more. Nagoya had no shortage to choose from, and the flavor of the month was, ironically, Oktoberfest. The festival was taking place throughout mid-July in Hisaya Ōdori Park, near Sakae. I reached out to Audrey, mentioned cheap beer and German sausages, and suddenly had company.

Truthfully, I attended the festival with low expectations. Nagoya was in the middle of an unusual extension to the rainy season, which I had been led to believe would last only as late as the end of June. The clear skies looked promising, though, so I left my umbrella at home and boarded a train. Thus, I was doubly annoyed to arrive in Sakae alongside a full-blown summer squall, in direct opposition to the prediction of both Google's best scientists and my own two eyes.

Audrey had arrived at the park before me, so we met up in the early afternoon to buy drink tickets from the main tent. Having long since gotten used to $1 cans of festival beer, we were unpleasantly surprised to find that the same standard did not apply to imported craft microbrews. After purchasing our tickets, we grabbed a couple of drinks and sat down at a crowded table.

For many festivalgoers, it was clearly not their first attendance. There was an ongoing live performance by the lederhosen-clad Zoogut Party Band, and even the most casual attendees seemed to know the lyrics to every song. These were exclusively in German (with the curious exception of YMCA), making it all the more impressive.

The rain was relentless, but Japanese revelers are not so easily deterred. A few scattered dancers emerged from beneath the shelter of the covered tables, then several more, and then a cadre of attractive young women, undoubtedly tasked by the festival's organizers with keeping spirits high and flowing. After a few unintelligible drinking chants, which proved effective nonetheless, a full-fledged conga line formed in the park.

It eventually dissolved into several dozen smaller groups of soaking dancers who were more than happy to continue their sodden celebrations in the rain. We watched with amusement from the safety of our covered table while we nursed our first beers, then our second, and then our third. By the time the festival ended, we had both finished half a dozen drinks.

Speaking of the festival's end, it highlighted once more that Japanese customs can be a double-edged sword. The nation's signature punctuality, for example, is a blessing when meeting with friends or catching a bus. However, it was a real disappointment when people were dancing, music was playing, and the beer was flowing freely, then all of that abruptly ceased at 5:00 sharp. By 5:10, Audrey and I were asked to relinquish our seats, as the cleaning crew had only the tables left to put away.

It was still light outside when we left the park. The two of us weren't yet ready to let the day end and, having just talked about the newest Marvel release, decided to extend our afternoon with an impromptu trip to the movies. Since we were already downtown, the nearest theater was only a short subway ride away. By that point, we had both drunkenly navigated the metro system many times before, so we had no trouble purchasing our tickets and boarding the train. There we waited, alongside a dozen or so other Oktoberfest attendees.

A few stops later, a shout of "Audrey!" pierced through the murmur of the crowd. I looked up to see an elderly Japanese woman running toward the train at a break-neck (or, in this case, potentially break-hip) pace. She made it on just as the doors closed behind her, flushed and out of breath.

"Hello," she offered sheepishly, wincing under the gaze of the many eyes on her. Then, to me, she added, "I'm Ayumi. Nice to meet you."

"She's a student of mine," Audrey explained. I became acutely aware of the alcohol on my breath.

Thankfully, it seemed Ayumi was blissfully unaware of our intoxication. I was impressed by her fluency as we spoke, as well as her outspokenness. The vast majority of my students (particularly those of the more aged persuasion) tended to be painfully reticent.

We chatted pleasantly for a few minutes until we reached Ayumi's stop. She said her goodbyes and got off of the train.

"Thank God," Audrey exhaled, along with a hearty lungful of hops. "I hope she couldn't tell we've been drinking. She's such a sweet, innocent lady."

That was the end of it, until two weeks later, when I received a call from Audrey.

"Hey Kyle, do you remember meeting Ayumi?" she asked. I confirmed that I did. "I taught her class today, and she mentioned when we ran into her in Sakae. I guess she had also been at Oktoberfest that morning, and she was worried we would notice she was drunk!"

Crisis averted, then. Back to the matter at hand.

The movie theater was tucked away in the back of a shopping mall, which, to me, sounded like the last desperate alliance of two industries that were quickly falling into obsolescence. Upon arriving, however, I realized I couldn't have been more mistaken.

To be clear, Japan has been at the forefront of innovation for the past half-century or so. It is the most technologically advanced nation in the world, bar none, and continues to distance itself from the competition by leaps and bounds every year. Accordingly, I was quite surprised to enter a 90s-era shopping mall and find thousands of people joyfully going about their business. Admittedly, this was a seven-story complex with all manner of retail stores and entertainment venues, but it was a far cry from the rapid decline of the American shopping center.

The movie theater was located in a separate entertainment center. It took a while to find, but we eventually did so with the assistance of a bemused security guard. Audrey and I purchased our tickets with about an hour to spare.

The theater's lobby was outlandishly Japanese. Life-sized Pokémon plushies adorned the walls, and four semi-private karaoke booths stood off to the side for moviegoers to enjoy as they waited for their movies to begin. Unfortunately, these were occupied, with a line to boot. We decided to go exploring.

An inexplicable fan-favorite amongst Japanese entertainment seekers is the crane game: that fraudulent relic from a bygone era of bowling alleys and laser tag. Somehow, it hasn't just survived the transition to digital media; it has flourished. So, when Audrey and I walked across the hall from the movie theater into a crane game emporium, it was not into a retro graveyard, as we expected, but a bustling arcade.

There were dozens of machines, beeping, whirling, and flashing with the attention-grabbing ferocity of a neon tempest. Each offered its own unique set of prizes, from knockoff jewelry to boot-leg game consoles. Lines had formed in some sections of the arcade, where players dutifully awaited their chance to be swindled by those machines offering the most coveted prizes: scantily-clad anime housewives, scantily-clad anime maids, and scantily-clad anime princesses.

Japan loves scantily-clad anime women.

Audrey and I tried to win a few of the tamer prizes, but we gave up after a dozen failed attempts. Defeated, the two of us made our way to the back of the game center, where a series of more traditional arcade games stood unused.

"What do you want to play?" I asked, looking around at the available options. The arcade had mostly racing and shooting games.

"Hmm, I don't mind anything so long as it isn't scary," Audrey replied.

As soon as she had spoken, a low groan cut across the room from behind. We spun around to discover the source of this sound: The House of the Dead IV.

We spun back around and locked eyes.

"It doesn't look too scary," I lied, blatantly.

Audrey sighed. "You know what? Let's give it a go." We each inserted 100 yen and pressed "Play."

Never before have I played a game with so many carnal jump-scares, nor so enjoyed a friend's bloodcurdling shrieks of terror. By the time we finished, I was doubled over with laughter, nearly in tears, and Audrey had frightened herself sober.

"That was so bad," she said, suppressing giggles.

"Want to go again?" I asked.

She declined.

Shortly after that, I received a notification that our movie was about to begin. Somehow, we had lost track of time amongst the many flashing lights. We made our way back through the entertainment complex to the theater.

In truth, the movie itself was the least interesting part of the entire experience. When all was said and done, we ended up enjoying the theater and its surroundings more than anything.

Afterward, Audrey and I parted ways for the night, satisfied that we had experienced another peculiarity of Japanese culture.

# Mt. Fuji

I n the months after arriving in Japan, I'd steadily checked several dozen items off my bucket list. I had experienced many aspects of Japanese culture that I had originally set out to see, from ancient mountain temples to sprawling city-wide festivals, as well as hundreds of others that I hadn't even known existed. However, due to its limited seasonal availability, one item had remained woefully unchecked: ascending Mt. Fuji.

Clocking in at a respectable 3,776 meters (12,390 feet), Mt. Fuji is the tallest mountain in Japan and the seventh-highest island peak on Earth. This makes it a popular destination for tourists and natives alike, who flock to the dormant, snow-capped volcano in their hundreds of thousands every year.

Mt. Fuji is the foremost of Japan's *sanreizan,* or Three Holy Mountains. It is particularly revered by those of the Shinto faith, as it is said to be the home of Konohanasakuya-hime, the patron goddess of volcanos. A rather fiery *kami,* Sakuya-hime (as she is also known) has a temper befitting her volcanic patronage. In one legend, she set fire to a hut while giving birth inside of it, enraged by her husband's accusations of infidelity. In another, she leveled the distant Yatsugatake mountain range for having the audacity to be taller than Mt. Fuji. Whether this is the result of a divine temper tantrum or simply the passage of time, the range now stands notably lower than Mt. Fuji at around 2,900 meters.

Shrines to Sakuya-hime have been built near the base of Mt. Fuji, in the hope that she will prevent the mountain from erupting further. Although the mountain has indeed remained dormant since the Hōei eruption of the early 1700s, the carbonized remains of similar shrines can be found littering Mount

Kirishima (one of Japan's most active volcanic sites). Thus, the effectiveness of Sakuya-hime's blessing remains in question.

Trevor, Audrey, and I—who had, by this point, become an inseparable trio of diehard adventurers—had talked about climbing Mt. Fuji in the abstract, but we had never laid any concrete plans. However, as the summer dragged on and our window of opportunity began to slowly swing closed, I tossed out a series of potential dates to gauge their interest. Their response was resoundingly positive, so we met to solidify our plans.

The planning stage was surprisingly simple, consisting of a two-hour meeting and a few jotted notes. Our group had long since proven to be a flexible, easygoing lot, which made the process very straightforward. We ironed out the details for transportation and housing with a few quick phone calls and agreed on a time and place to meet.

Our journey began after work on a Saturday with a night bus to the base of the mountain. We arrived at the bus stop earlier than was strictly necessary due to a chronic history of missing our transport when traveling together. As doing so would have proved a rather insurmountable setback in this case, we made sure to pad our plans with more than enough spare time to account for any likely holdups. This, of course, ended up being the first time in six months that we all arrived on time, leaving us with heavy packs and an hour to kill.

Since we'd all just completed a full day's work and not yet eaten, we were feeling a bit peckish. We checked out the many nutritionally substantive restaurants available within the station, perfect for the eve of a great departure, before making our way to McDonald's for some toe-curling, artery-clogging goodness. After scarfing down 1,200 calories in the space of ten minutes, and fully in the throes of a tryptophan-induced stupor, we went to pick up our tickets and wait in line for the bus.

There we met a rather ebullient traveler from Hong Kong, who had the hot vinegar stench of a well-traveled man, long unwashed. And although we spent several hours engaged in intimate conversation with him, I cannot recall his name for the life of me. Thus, the man I will hereafter refer to as Hong informed us that he had been traveling around Japan for several weeks as part of a marathon trip across Asia. He had recently come from Myanmar, via the Philippines, and soon planned to embark for South Korea. I know all of this because he told me as much, completely unbidden, within the first thirty seconds of making his acquaintance.

Mr. Kong was the exact sort of man that I had dreaded sitting next to on an overnight bus: pleasant to the point where I felt the need to reciprocate, but seemingly oblivious to all but the most blatant of social cues. Once he began talking about his travels, he was unstoppable, pausing only to noisily suck in lungfuls of air. He maintained a seamless, stream-of-consciousness monologue, which thankfully required very little input on our part.

"I went to Dubai for three weeks, then to New Delhi for seven. I was supposed to stay in New Delhi for eight weeks, but the rain drove me off early. After that, I took a trip to Nepal—have you been to Nepal?" He occasionally peppered in these rhetorical questions to maintain the pretense of a bilateral conversation. Had I been the Nepali heir apparent, however, he would have remained none the wiser, as he would continue without pause. "Anyway, you should go there. I tried to visit Mt. Everest, too, but it was too cold. I did meet a nice Sherpa by the name of..." and so on (and on).

He eventually tuckered himself out, presumably from self-imposed hypoxia, but not before he'd robbed us of several precious hours of pre-hike slumber. Afterward, the overnight bus's unreclining seats and inexplicably talkative driver did their best to deprive us of the rest.

Several hours of fitful quasi-sleep later, the bus arrived in Kawaguchiko, a small town near the base of the mountain. Raring to get started, we chartered one more bus to the Fuji Subaru Line Fifth Station, approximately 2,300 meters up the sacred mountain.

The Fifth Station is the last bastion of comfort available to climbers before they embark upon their journey. It's flashy, excessive, and designed solely to relieve you of any cumbersome pocket change before you set out—truly, it's a public service. It's

*Target acquired*

also a sightseeing attraction in its own right, offering a panoramic view of the northern landscape for those who may not wish to brave the mountain proper.

*Not a bad view to start the day*

Due to the risk posed by altitude sickness (and doubtless the quiet insistence of the resident store owners), the official recommendation is to spend at least one hour at the station while your body acclimates. Being obedient consumers, and in desperate need of caffeine, we spent this time drinking coffee and eating Fuji-shaped melon bread. We also spent some time at a nearby lookout point.

I've spoken before about the sheer, unadulterated joy of returning to nature after time spent in the city. It's the chest-loosening thrill of an open trail and eager feet, or the crunch of autumn leaves underfoot. It's at once intimately familiar and wondrously novel, each and every time that it's experienced anew.

Gazing down on civilization from afar, and from above, is something more remarkable still. Distance forces a change of perspective: If the mountains below seem so inconsequential, and they, in turn, dwarf the cities beneath, how important can the problems of the people within those cities truly be?

Audrey and I made a quick pit stop at the mountain shrine to add to our growing stamp collections. Then, the three of us set our boots to the trail. (Or, in Audrey's case, sandals. Yes, she hiked Mt. Fuji in camp sandals.)

Our opinions on the weather fluctuated wildly that first day. When we'd arrived in Kawaguchiko that morning, it was already pushing 90° Fahrenheit (32° C)—an ungodly temperature at 8:00 AM, even for a Japanese summer. However, after the charter bus had deposited us at the Fifth Station, we were relieved to discover that the change in altitude had granted a balmier, more arid quality to the previously sweltering heat.

This relief lasted only a few minutes once we began walking. The tree cover thinned out, then vanished entirely, and the realization set in that it would be just *this,* under the beating sun, until we reached our destination. The three of us played word games for a short while—the enthralling recreation of English teachers—but these fizzled out as breathing in became preferable to speaking out. It had also become clear that I was both under-equipped and over-packed, which further contributed to my weariness. While I'd declined to pack proper hiking boots, I had somehow found it entirely reasonable to bring three changes of clothing for our two-day trip.

We set an ambitious pace to start, fueled as we were by caffeine and excitement. After arriving at the Sixth Station (an hour's walk from the Fifth, by most estimates) in thirty minutes flat, we decided to slow down. Of course, "decided" might be a misleading word. It may be more apt to say that our carefree enthusiasm was replaced by a sense of cautious optimism, then quiet resignation. We had nothing to do but walk until we reached our hut for the night, and all that awaited us there was the promise of shelter and a chance to lie down.

This became a more alluring promise the longer we trekked, but after a while, we fell into a sort of comfortable rhythm: left, right, left, right, stop. Marvel at the sheer beauty of your surroundings. Try to capture it with a picture. Fail. Drink some water. Inwardly reflect that you're going through it too quickly, then drink some more anyway, because it's hot and you're weak-willed. Continue onwards: left, right.

So our time elapsed, past the Sixth Station, and then the Seventh. We shared a few memorable moments along the way—most notably, as we were sitting along a rocky outcropping, griping about the impossibility of scaling a mountain in two days' time, only for a gaggle of jovial schoolchildren to skip merrily by—but our time was largely spent in companionable silence. Even as the terrain twisted sharply upward past the Seventh Station, shifting abruptly from the humdrum monotony of switchbacks to an outright scramble, it did little to break us out of our reverie.

*The going gets tough*

It may come as no surprise, then, that we passed our hut entirely. After nearly five hours of hiking, all three of us shook alert at once to discover that we had reached Horai-kan—one hut past our own. While we had only climbed perhaps five extra minutes, it had been a particularly arduous stretch, and we were greatly discouraged by the prospect of reliving it in reverse.

Defeated, the three of us sat down on a small stone ledge in front of Horai-kan. The plan was to rest our feet before climbing down, but it quickly developed the risk of becoming an unwelcome nap. As "dangling precariously over a yawning abyss" is perhaps the least appropriate time to fall asleep, we reluctantly descended back along the twice-accursed path to our hut.

We found our accommodation rather spartan but entirely adequate. There was a large entranceway, one small dining room, and a half-dozen smaller sleeping areas. These each contained rows of tightly-packed bedrolls, which were laid out on the hardwood floor. After a brief tour ("Sleep here, urinate there. Money, please."), we passed out on our bedrolls for a much-needed nap, too weary to even crawl inside of them.

Our hostess woke us up around 3:00 PM for dinner. A bowl of steaming curry was served in the dining room, along with a chunk of rock-hard bread. "One hot and a wooden slab" is a far cry from the old lodging standard, but we appreciated it nonetheless.

Following dinner, we returned to our designated sleeping area for some more shut-eye. The plan was to sleep for eight hours, then rally at midnight to continue our journey. As I am neither infirm nor a child, however, my body firmly refused to fall asleep at 4:00 PM. After several hours of reading and a few short walks along the rapidly cooling mountainside, I surrendered myself to the sleepless night ahead.

Around 11:30 PM, our bunkmates—who were separated from us by about three inches and a thin linen sheet—began to rouse. By that point, I was bored practically to tears and desperately wanted to get moving. I began to not-so-subtly suggest as much to my sleeping companions, who, after a few pointed coughs in their general direction, begrudgingly stirred.

Mt. Fuji's second stretch is traditionally hiked in the dead of night, under cover of stars and little else. Those who are willing to wake early and push through their exhaustion are rewarded with a singular view of the sun rising from nearly two and a half miles above sea level.

The previous night's dining room had been converted into additional sleeping space, so there was no room inside to eat our breakfast. The three of us put on several layers of clothing, took one step outside, and immediately stepped back inside to add several more. It was *cold*: the kind of deep, biting cold that laughs at your ineffectual windbreaker as it cuts through in search of the tender flesh beneath. Even with enough layers to give Randy from A Christmas Story a waddle for his money, I spent all of breakfast shivering. Trevor and Audrey fared little better; so, when even three piping hot cups of coffee failed to alleviate the chill, we decided to get moving. The remaining hike was supposedly the steepest and most strenuous portion, and we had joyous expectations about the body heat that we would soon generate.

The previous day's hike had seen a haphazard assortment of eager travelers clambering over and past one another to reach their destinations. As we began our starlit ascent, however, the trail narrowed out considerably, funneling the remaining hikers into one orderly, weary procession.

*The tough get going*

Trevor, Audrey, and I climbed together in silence. The movement kept us warm for the most part, but the longer we climbed, the more sluggish we became. Around 2:00 AM, our strength began to wane. The trail of headlamps seemed to stretch immeasurably upward, and the summit itself seemed to remain impossibly far away at all times.

Due to our inability to read basic signage, we several times thought ourselves to be closer to the peak than we actually were. After having our hopes dashed a few times in this manner, we eventually identified the end of our climb by a series of blinking red lights at the summit.

Once, when I was a younger man, my brothers and I took a self-guided road trip around Iceland's Ring Road. On the fourth day of our journey, we foolishly decided to visit a crashed DC-3 US Navy airplane that lay along the black sand beaches of Sólheimasandur. The plane was clearly visible from the road, barely a few minutes' walk away, yet it maddeningly maintained that distance despite several hours of walking directly toward it.

The red lights at Mt. Fuji's peak followed the same reality-defying physics. No matter how many times I turned my gaze skyward, toward the summit and its vast indifference, they refused to shift from their original position. In fact, as time went on, they seemed to recede even farther into the distance. I began to see them as twinkling eyes, mocking us for our utter lack of progression.

That said, it's incredible what strength can be found in having a singular purpose. By the most charitable of estimates, we had each gotten four hours of sleep on the initial bus ride over. Combined with my staggering zero hours at the mountain hut, this brought my average to two hours in as many nights. Still, I felt acutely awake. Maybe flooding itself with adrenaline was my body's way of begging me to get to a place where each new breath didn't wrack my body with icy shudders, but I was alert and present. All around me, I could see this same sentiment reflected in the faces of our fellow travelers: physically exhausted, but fiercely determined.

Of course, this strength was little more than a finite bit of chemical delusion. It was the foolhardy assuredness of a child on Christmas Eve, certain that they will stay awake to meet Santa Claus, simply because of how strongly they want to do so. And as they inevitably discover—waking up the next morning tucked snuggly into bed with smirking parents and a host of presents under the tree—it couldn't last forever.

I reached that point approximately 15 minutes from the summit, when our journey was all but complete. My eyelids grew heavy, and my feet heavier still, until it seemed they would no longer obey my pleading instructions to carry me to the top. The taunting flicker of the lights at the summit snapped abruptly into imminent view, as if from a camera focusing, but I found myself exhausted. Only the flow of the crowd kept me moving onward and upward toward the peak.

As we entered the final stretch, mountain rangers appeared along the trail, frantically yelling out the distance to the top. Fifteen minutes. Ten minutes. Five minutes.

Summit.

I wish I could write now about the elation I felt as we crested that final peak, or wax poetic about the sense of oneness experienced from gazing down at a moonlit world from above, but I simply cannot. In truth, all that I felt as the ground leveled out beneath us was relief. As an old Japanese proverb states: "A wise man climbs Fuji once. Only a fool climbs it twice."

Together, we staggered toward the golden glow of the summit's vending machines (the highest point in Japan is, after all, still Japan) and purchased some piping hot coffee. As I felt it scalding its way through my system, Trevor, Audrey, and I wandered toward one of two functioning restaurants at the summit. It was ostensibly just three paper-thin walls and a roof containing rows of benches and the chance for a bowl of steaming liquid, but at that moment, it was a serpent-less Eden.

*Lookin' like a dead man walking*

Once the collective body heat of the poor souls huddled around us had worked its way into our bones, we gathered our scattered belongings and wits to brave the elements on the mountain-top once more. There was still approximately half an hour until sunrise, but people were already beginning to claim their positions near the cliff face. We made our way forward through the crowd, gradually replacing each consecutive person who surrendered to the cold, until we had reached the front. There we waited, equal parts miserable and excited.

To me, the beauty in a sunrise has never been in the sun actually rising. It is in the moments beforehand, as the whole world seems to wait with bated breath, and the sky is painted in resplendent pastels. It is simply indescribable, so I will attempt to do so no further. All that I can say is this: As the first streak of brilliant orange crept up from the horizon, I was ecstatic. It felt as if our entire climb had culminated in this moment—watching the sunrise from the atop the heavens, bathing the sleepy mountains below in the light of a new day.

After the sun had risen, the three of us explored for a bit at the top of the mountain. A quick peek into the caldera confirmed that it was dormant, much to our relief. None of us much relished the idea of having reached our goal only to be precipitously Pompeii-ed. We took another long moment to bask in the glory of our achievement, then began our descent.

This, I should have remembered from prior climbing expeditions in my Boy Scouting days, is always deceptively unpleasant. We had been aware that we would need to climb down the mountain at some point, of course, but hadn't given it much thought from a practical standpoint. So strongly had tunnel vision set in during the final stages of our hike, with the sun itself promising light at the end of it, that we hadn't mentally accounted for much beyond the summit.

If the ascent had been exactly as we had hoped—arduous, exciting, and wonderfully rewarding—the descent was anything but. Rather, it was grueling, repetitive, and (worst of all) *boring*. The journey upward had been just that: a journey. It had seen us alternating between switchbacks, stairways, and scrambling for several hours at a time. Any time that we began to grow bored of the terrain, it would change entirely.

The descent, however, amounted to four and a half hours of identical switchbacks. Period. Back, forth, back, forth, until the sun reached its zenith and beyond. Worse still, the trail itself was made of loose gravel, which ensured that we never truly found our footing. It was perversely reminiscent of ice skating, in a way: place one foot, slide several meters. Place the other, slide several more.

This could have been quite therapeutic, had the unstable footing not caused us each to fall every couple of minutes. We began taking turns wiping out, in an effort to appease the gods of gravity-induced rectal pain, but they cared little for our plight. By the time we reached to the Fifth Station, our tailbones and pride were both mortally wounded.

But, reach the Fifth Station we eventually did. Such little of interest occurred during the interim hours that I quite simply could not write more about if I wanted to. For those who are planning to hike Mt. Fuji and have casually dismissed the many warnings about injuries on the way down: Reconsider your life choices, and bring a walking stick.

Our return journey faded into the blur of the mundane experienced after something phenomenal. Presumably, we purchased bus tickets back to Kawaguchiko, then train tickets homeward from there, but my memories of this are hazy at best. We arrived in Nagoya in the late afternoon and parted ways. I closed my eyes for a short nap just before 7:00 PM, then awoke nearly 16 hours later to the light of a new day.

# Obon

One week after I had climbed Mt. Fuji, my wonderful brothers all took a break from their busy lives to visit me in Japan. This was their first time in Japan, and, after half a year, I had enough of a grasp on my daily life that I was excited to show them around my new home. Although our itinerary was essentially the same as my parents' trip in April, the execution and outcome promised to be significantly different.

For starters, there are three of them, all varying degrees of "large" compared to the Japanese populace. They were staying in my 208-square-foot apartment for the first two nights, and the four of us plus their luggage consumed about half of that space.

But, I'm getting ahead of myself. My brothers' Japanese experience began before I had even returned home from work on the first night to greet them. While they were passed out on my living room floor, exhausted from their 12-hour flight, there came a knock at my door. My younger brother Patrick, who was deliriously tired and couldn't speak a single word of Japanese, deemed himself qualified to answer it. He was greeted by the Buddhist equivalent of Jehovah's Witnesses: two elderly women, armed with multilingual pamphlets, hoping to proselytize nonbelievers through the threat of damnation. Unfortunately for them, Buddhism's "animalistic reincarnation" isn't quite as sexy of a punishment as the Judaic "eternal hellfire," so they had their work cut out for them.

One of the ladies asked Patrick in faltering English whether he was Christian. He confirmed that he was. By his recounting, what then followed was thirty uninterrupted seconds of the two ladies yelling, "No, Buddha, Buddha, Buddha!" before he awkwardly let the door swing shut in their faces.

This must not have left much of an impression on him, though, as they were all sound asleep again by the time I came home from work that night. I roused them in the gentlest, most brotherly way possible (blasting DMX's timeless "X Gon' Give it to Ya" through my Bluetooth speakers), and we said our hellos. After forcing them to get ready for a night out—akin to mobilizing an army, in both the time and effort required—we left to meet my friends and co-workers at karaoke.

My brothers had sung karaoke before, at the odd sports bar and honky-tonk in America. That said, there's nothing quite like your first experience in a Japanese parlor. For starters, we were surprised to find that they had given Felicity and Fumika—two diminutive women—the Party Deluxe Room, which could have easily housed the aforementioned army. It was also nearly impossible to be shy around my Japanese co-workers, who were shamelessly uninhibited when it came to singing. If they could belt out the lyrics to "Don't Stop Me Now" in their second language, we could sure as hell try it in our first.

*From left to right: Joe, Patrick, and Connor*

As per usual, we extended our two-hour reservation to three hours, then four, then to the "Whatever, You're Already Here" package. We finally left the room around sunrise with sore throats and busy livers. My brothers and I returned to my apartment and crashed.

The next morning, we woke up at 9:00 AM sharp. Growing up, I had always bemoaned my father's insistence on waking us up early on vacation ("We're burning daylight!"). It's vacation; why not relax? But as with a great many things, I've come to see the wisdom of his ways. I had about five days' worth of activities planned for our two nights in Nagoya, and I was damned sure that sleeping past noon wasn't one of them.

Luckily, my brothers were all good sports. After taking showers—the first of many on this trip—we boarded a series of trains bound for Inuyama Castle. Unfortunately, having graciously decided not to burn daylight, we discovered that daylight was unwilling to return the favor.

That first day was nearly 105° Fahrenheit (40.5° Celsius), and that was only the beginning of the season's hottest week. We arrived at Inuyama Station around midday, which meant there was little shade to cower in as we made our way to the castle. By the time we arrived at the gate, we were already drenched in sweat, shirts moist and hair matted to our foreheads. The castle was under repair, limiting visitors to the first three floors. Thankfully, those floors were outside of the sun's merciless reach, so we took shelter within the castle as in days of old.

As I mentioned during my previous visit, Inuyama Castle is one of Japan's oldest. It sits atop a small hill overlooking the Kiso River, and the historic shopping streets at its base offers visitors a chance to feel as if they have stepped backward in time to when it was first constructed. My brothers and I set off through these streets in search of a replacement for the several pounds of salt we had shed throughout the morning. We eventually stumbled upon a courtyard of sorts, which contained several food trucks and the incessant buzzing of a dozen air conditioning units struggling valiantly against the elements.

We surveyed the available options from the paltry shelter of a gauzy white canopy. The chefs regarded us warily, clearly not thrilled by the prospect of adding the heat of their stoves to that of the sun. We eventually settled on *yakisoba* and *karaage*, my personal favorites (or, as I presented it to my brothers, must-have local delicacies), and sat down to wait.

As our eyes drifted lazily about the square, they were drawn by the liberal use of punctuation to one particularly excitable sign, which offered "long fries." While "length" is not a quality that I would typically look for in fries, the sign's precise wording ("LONG!!! LONG!!! YEAAAAH!!! YEAAAAH!!! YEAAAAH!!!") enticed my brothers and me to buy some all the same.

To be fair, they were some outrageously long fries.

Once we had replenished our sodium reserves, we returned to my apartment to take our second showers of the day. (Or, rather, my brothers did. I had long since surrendered myself the Church of Eternal Perspiration and could no longer be bothered to wash more than once per day.) Afterward, we settled in for an evening at home. Between jet-lag and dehydration, my brothers were wiped out, and I wasn't far behind.

On the third morning of our trip, we made an impromptu decision to visit Osu Kannon: the famous local temple known for its nearby traditional shopping district. As one of a few noteworthy sites within the city that I had yet to see, it promised to be a novel experience for all. In truth, however, it was nearby, and we were simply wary of any excursion that would take us more than thirty minutes from the guaranteed shelter of my apartment.

By the time we arrived in the Osu shopping district, the streets were already bustling with activity. Shoppers of all ages and ethnicities crowded the streets, stopping often to drop into the street's many restaurants and cafes; and boy, does Japan love a good themed cafe.

Besides the more innocuous varieties—like cat cafes, where customers can enjoy the company of friendly felines while they eat—Japanese cafes also cater to more exotic and erotic tastes. Within Osu alone, there is an owl cafe, a rabbit cafe, and any number of maid cafes, where wealthy patrons can pay exorbitant fees to be lavished with attention by young women dressed à la French au pairs. Although there is nothing explicitly sexual about this service, that's not to say that prostitution doesn't exist within Japan.

Japan's *fūzoku*—sex trade—industry is still very much alive, supported by an abundance of legal loop-holes and the pseudo-legitimized Yakuza crime syndicate. Without delving too deeply into any particulars, Japanese authorities seem to adhere to the philosophy of "where there's a will, there's a way" and have fashioned laws to regulate the industry instead of attempting to abolish it outright.

Perhaps more prevalent in recent years, however, has been Japan's *mizu-shōbai*, or "water trade"—services designed to stimulate their clients' social needs rather than their sexual urges. You see, Japanese society as a whole is becoming progressively more withdrawn. Depression is at an all-time high, and nearly 1% of the population lives in the state of extreme self-imposed isolation known as *hikikomori*: a Japanese phenomenon where an individual refuses to leave their home for a period exceeding six months. The causes of this condition can vary, but they're usually some combination of Japan's unique and pervasive societal pressures. While Western media has undeniably overblown the importance of honor and shame in Japanese culture, they do play a significant role in determining one's path in life.

So, rather than engage in normal social discourse, which carries the risk of disappointment or humiliation, many people choose to pay for social companionship. This can include anything from the platonic engagement of the aforementioned maid cafes to the outright rental of an entire family.

So, then, back to Osu.

At that time, my brothers and I lacked the energy and wherewithal to enter any of these cafes. The trip itself was already a maiden voyage for my brothers, so we declined to embark on another, as it were. We ducked into a few shops as we walked along the covered pedestrian street, then made our way to the shrine. When we arrived, my youngest brother, Joe, remarked on how abruptly it had appeared: an entire shrine complex, materializing as if out of nowhere in the middle of a city block.

Ōsu Kannon, formally known as Kitanosan Shinpuku-ji Hōshō-in, is not the oldest temple in Japan, nor is it the most spectacular. Thankfully, that still leaves room for it to be remarkably both. Originally built around the turn of the 14th century, it was dedicated to a statue of Avalokiteśvara carved by Kukai, the father of Shingon Buddhism.

My older brother, Connor, had had the foresight to purchase a high-tech camera in preparation for their trip, and he put it to good use capturing the vibrant brilliance of the temple grounds. My brothers also took this opportunity to each purchase their own *goshuinchō*, which they would gradually add to over the course of the week.

After paying our respects at the temple, my brothers and I returned to my apartment. They took their second showers of the day, then the four of us packed our bags and left for Nagoya Station. We had tickets for an evening bullet train to Kyoto, and we couldn't afford to miss it.

## The Boys are Back in Town

The bullet train cut our 80-mile trip down to a mere thirty-five minutes. Once in Kyoto, we flagged down a taxi to take us to our hotel.

Per my brothers' request, we were staying at the rustic mountainside *ryokan* from my parents' visit. Getting there involved the same harrowing nighttime drive through the mountains as before. As an added coincidence, we had the same bilingual taxi driver as the first night of Golden Week—the one who had previously commented that the prospect of driving back from this hotel at night scared her.

Sorry, lady.

Having been forewarned that there would now be four large American men staying at the hotel, the proprietress had seen fit to procure four pairs of the Sasquatch slippers that they had previously given my father. We stumbled over these a half-dozen times on the way up to our room.

There, we changed into the decorative *yukatas* that awaited us. In the process of doing so, we each knocked our heads a half-dozen times against a low-hanging wooden beam that stretched directly across the center of the room. Perhaps when the hotel was built, a few hundred years ago, it was of an appropriate height; in the modern era, however, it served only to concuss.

Once properly adorned, we went downstairs for dinner. Due to the temperature indoors, dinner was served outside on a small veranda beside the river. (Most traditional Japanese buildings have been retrofitted with central air, but the lack of modern insulation makes it a stopgap at best.) The cool night air and the soporific flicker of the veranda's paper lanterns made for a truly magical atmosphere in which to enjoy our meal.

The fermented fish heads that were served with our first course did little to further the effect.

When my parents had returned home from their visit in April, they had shared pictures with my brothers of all the culinary curiosities that they had eaten: whole-squid sushi, fish heads, and the like. While they had been good sports at the time, Patrick and Joe were considerably less adventurous. Patrick, in particular—who, in his daily life, avoids even the most thoroughly cooked of seafood—was particularly unenthused.

"In fairness," I pointed out as Patrick prodded at his fish head with the tip of a chopstick, "we are staying at a riverside hotel. They were bound to have some river fish."

"Yeah," he replied, "but that doesn't mean I have to eat it." He looked at me imploringly. "Does it?"

Joe was less vocal about his grievances, but he may have simply been too busy choking down bile to complain.

Their discomfort provided Connor and me with enough entertainment to get through our own courses with relative ease. Each new fish-laden dish brought on an eruption of laughter from our table, as they struggled to conceal their disgust.

After the second course, the owner herself came to collect the trays from our table. She looked crestfallen to see Patrick's food still untouched, and I, not wanting to further offend the staff at my favorite hotel, resolved to eat the remainder of each of his dishes. This was no problem at first, as the majority of the food was truly delicious. For the fourth course, however, the owner returned with what can only be described as a festering tray of putrid mudfish. Thin, scaly, and reeking of fermentation gone wrong, the poor creature's eyes had begun to deliquesce, oozing from the fractured remnants of its skull.

"I'm not eating that," Patrick said as soon as the hostess had left earshot.

*No worries,* I thought, *that was to be expected. I can choke down two of these.*

"Me neither," Joe chimed.

I turned to Connor, heart dropping as I saw revulsion written plainly across his face. "Sorry, Ky," he added apologetically. "I can't do it."

Betrayed by my kin, I steeled myself and took a bite.

In their defense, it was truly revolting. The fish was gritty and pasty, with skin like sandpaper. In a failed attempt to mask the stench of river mud, they had doused it in an overpowering alcohol marinade that made it difficult to inhale too deeply while eating. The overall effect was quite similar, I imagine, to downing a lit can of Sterno filled with innumerable tiny bones. By the time I made it to the head of my fish, even I didn't have the strength to continue. I slowly picked away at Patrick's over the remainder of the meal but didn't make much progress. My only reward was a faint glimmer of satisfaction in the stewardess's eyes when she came to collect our trays once more—along with what looked suspiciously like wry amusement. After dinner, the four of us returned to our room and cracked open a bottle of sake from the mini-fridge. We took our time drinking it beneath the decadent comfort of the room's air conditioning.

The next morning, we awoke to another scorcher. Our first plan was to visit the nearby mountain temples of Jingoji, Saimyoji, and Kosanji.

Jingoji, the ancient mountain temple that I had visited with my parents during Golden Week, is situated atop Takao Mountain and can only be reached via several hundred mossy stone steps behind our hotel. While this climb had proved an enjoyable challenge in April, it was nearly unbearable in August. We found ourselves pausing every dozen steps or so to catch our breath. Of course, when we finally reached the summit, it was worth the effort. The fresh mountain air, alongside the temple's proud austerity, made for potent nostalgia indeed.

We briefly stopped at the other two temples, after Jingoji. Saimyoji was quaint, if a bit unremarkable, and Kosanji, an expansive UNESCO World Heritage Site, was undergoing major renovations. However, at Kosanji, we were able to take a peek at the *Chōjū-jinbutsu-giga*, or Scrolls of Frolicking Animals. The first of these four scrolls, dating back to the 12th century, is widely considered the original Japanese manga.

From Kosanji, we returned to our hotel to call a taxi to the city. Takeshi, an outgoing staff member in his early 30s, overheard our request and intervened, offering to drive us to the nearest train station. We took him up on this generous offer and soon piled into his featureless white van.

Takeshi and I made what little small talk we could with our sparse shared vocabulary. My brothers sat in appreciative silence. However, about five minutes into the drive, we encountered a roadblock: another featureless white van, idling alongside the narrow country road, making it impossible to pass.

Takeshi gave his horn a polite press. He made as if to say something to us, then settled for an apologetic shrug.

"Huh," Joe noted as we waited for the van to move, "it's filled with old people." Upon further inspection, we noticed that he was correct: Every seat was occupied by an elderly man or woman—except for the driver's seat, which remained conspicuously vacant.

Takeshi made a sound somewhere between a grunt and a sigh. His face betrayed no emotion, but he gave the horn a slightly lengthier, less polite press. We continued waiting.

Thirty seconds later, he sighed and placed our van in park. He got out with a bitterly muttered "*kuso*" (an expletive that is best left untranslated).

"What's he doing?" Patrick asked.

"I'm not sure," I replied as he approached the other van. "Maybe he's going to ask them where the driver is?"

Any notion of such a mundane solution was dispelled as he reached the driver's side door, opened it, and proceeded to clamber inside. The six elderly faces behind him went from placid delirium to alarm in 0.5 seconds flat, as the suave stranger who had commandeered their vehicle began to drive away.

Thankfully, Takeshi only drove up the road a few meters before parking once more where the street widened out. He hopped back out of the van (to its passengers' immense relief) and returned to ours. We continued on our merry way.

While this entire exchange lasted only two minutes, perhaps, it did impart a valuable lesson in Japanese etiquette:

JPY 101: The legendary patience of Japanese waitstaff does not extend to situations that inconvenience their customers.

I only wish we had been able to see the actual driver of the other van as he emerged from some nearby building to find his vehicle parked ten meters from where he had left it, filled with bewildered seniors.

We reached the station without further incident shortly after noon and caught a local train from there into the city. We then met up with another group for a sightseeing bike tour, similar to the one that I had taken with my parents. We visited all of the same sights, ending with an afternoon ride through the Gion geisha district.

"What should we do now?" Connor asked after we had returned our bikes. We were sitting in the shade of a nearby maple tree, whose broad leaves provided our first shelter of the afternoon. None of us particularly wanted to return to our hotel for dinner, as it was quite a ways from the city proper, and doing so would have signaled an end to the day's activities.

While we were sitting there, mulling over our choices for the afternoon, we heard the familiar lilting melody of festival music in the distance. Drawn by the potential for a cold beverage like silk moths to a paper lantern, we set off on foot through the streets of northern Kyoto. The afternoon heat had begun to dissipate, but we were still drenched in sweat from the bike ride. Our next stop was sure to be the evening's last.

We arrived at the melody's source, in one of the district's many alleyways, to find hundreds of people crowded around a raised dais. A slow, spiraling dance took place around the dais, led by four geishas on the platform.

Bon Odori is a folk dance performed during Obon, the weeklong holiday during which my brothers visited. The dance welcomes the spirits of the dead, who are traditionally held to visit their descendants during this somber holiday. Each region of Japan has its own variation of the dance, as do China, Vietnam, and Korea, who celebrate similar Buddhist holidays of the same origin.

We stayed at the festival until sunset, basking in the strangely reserved energy of the festivities. People danced slowly, spoke in hushed tones, and sweat profusely. Afterward, my brothers and I stopped at an Indian restaurant for some spicy curry—for all that we complained about the heat, we're gluttons for punishment—before retiring to our hotel for the night.

The fifth day of our trip was cooler (or, at least, slightly less sweltering) and full of promise. My brothers and I scarfed down our hotel breakfast in a matter of minutes (Patrick still carefully avoiding anything that resembled seafood) and set out for the day. We made our way to Kyoto Station, and from there caught a bullet train into the neighboring city of Nara.

Nara, a popular tourist city founded in the 8th century AD, is home to many attractions. Besides the plethora of temples and shrines that any self-respecting Japanese city can lay claim to, they also have several *kofun*—ancient Japanese burial mounds—stemming from Nara's stint as the nation's capital from 710 to 784 AD. Chief among its religious sites are the *Nanto Shichi Daiji*: seven Buddhist temples of particular cultural and historical significance. These include Todaiji Temple—the world's largest wooden building—and Kōfukuji, which is famous for its five-story pagoda. Perhaps Nara's most notable attraction, however, is its park, which is home to nearly 1,600 wild sika deer.

According to legend, Nara's spotted deer have been revered as protectors of the realm since the thunder god Takemikazuchi-no-Mikoto traveled to Nara on a white stag to guard the newly-established capital. While some may choose to doubt this story, killing one of the city's holy protectors remained punishable by death until 1637.

These days, the deer have been stripped of their sacred designation but retain their status as a collective national treasure. They are allowed to roam freely within the park, unimpeded—and often pampered—by the park's 13 million annual visitors. In 2017, a surge in their population led to a government-sanctioned culling of those deer unfortunate enough to stray too far from their designated habitat. Since then, the remaining deer have learned to stay close to the visitors.

And they are certainly majestic beasts in person. We made our way directly from Nara Station to the park, pausing only briefly to pick up some *sembei:* brittle rice crackers that visitors can—in theory—feed by the handful to hundreds of eagerly awaiting deer. Unfortunately, the truth was a bit less remarkable.

We arrived at the park in the early afternoon to find that the deer had already been well-fed that day, as well as every other day since birth. Groups of obese, shit-flecked doe waddled aimlessly about, followed by a handful of cantankerous, overheating bucks. Hordes of gibbering tourists swarmed in their wake, thrusting unbidden crackers in their faces. Most of these advances were met with weary indifference, but occasionally a tourist would overstep and receive a cautionary grunt from a nearby buck.

While they were generally uninterested in the crackers, the deer were more than happy to accept gifts of water from any visitors generous enough to provide. In one horrifying incident, we saw a young boy with charitable intent and murderous execution stuffing his upended bottle down a doe's throat, her wide eyes frenzied as she struggled to consume the bottle's contents.

My brothers and I, too, tried our best to find a photogenic moment of interspecies companionship, but most of our crackers were eaten by reluctant stragglers. However, after twenty minutes, we spotted a herd of particularly spritely deer emerging from a restricted area across the park. We made our way over as inconspicuously as possible for four white giants in a sea of middling Asian tourists, careful not to draw any attention toward the new arrivals. There we found what we had been hoping for: a hungry buck, willing to bow his head in exchange for a cracker.

*A buck emerging from the restricted area*

You see, the sacred deer of Nara Park have learned to imitate the deferential mannerisms of their bipedal neighbors to great effect. And, while this sounds quite touching in theory—two proud and noble species sharing a moment of mutual respect—in reality, it imparts with a sudden sense of clarity that this mild-mannered ruminant herbivore is equipped with a skull full of knives at the exact height of a human groin. Indeed, in the 2017 fiscal year alone, at least 164 visitors to the park were injured or maimed by overzealous bucks.

One particularly aggressive newcomer seemed aware that we had food. He sniffed at our shorts, prodding inquisitively with his nose; I, fearing disembowelment, gave him the rest of my crackers. He rewarded me with one brief bow for doing so.

*Anyone paying particularly close attention to this photo might notice that my groin is held farther back than strictly necessary*

Having consumed our remaining *sembei*, the buck and his entourage moved on in search of further tourists to bully. Our objective similarly complete, we wandered the grounds a while longer before heading south a short ways to Kofukuji Temple. There, I added a 30-something[th] stamp to my *goshuinchō*, while my brothers took shelter in the shade of a nearby building. By then, the endless, oppressive heat was beginning to take its toll once more, so we returned to Kyoto via the *shinkansen* for a brief nap.

That night, we planned to hike up Inari Mountain, along the *torii*-lined pathways of Fushimi Inari. As you might recall from my Golden Week adventure, this grand shrine boasts well over 30,000 vermillion *torii* gates. The largest of these are sponsored by wealthy benefactors, who believe the mountain god will grant them good fortune in return for their generosity. Of course, each benefactors' personal and business information is printed on the front of the gates themselves, adding a much more material benefit to the exchange.

On my previous visit, during the new emperor's coronation, the slow-moving, tightly-packed crowds had made scaling the mountain past a certain point nearly impossible; indeed, perhaps the only competent thing that our tour guide had done at the time was abort our climb in its early stages. However, at night, and in the throes of summer, the shrine promised to be far less crowded and, as such, offered a much more intimate experience for any would-be explorers.

The four of us arrived at Fushimi Inari five minutes before sunset: for once, exactly on time. We passed through the first grand *torii* just as the sun winked out beneath the horizon, leaving a swath of burnished gold in its wake.

As the last few rays of crimson bled from the horizon, so too did the majority of the shrine's worshipers shuffle out through the front gate. For good reason, it turned out—by day, Fushimi Inari is a place of vivid colors and vibrant energy. At night, however, it becomes an altogether gloomier place.

We located the trailhead and set off up the mountainside. The entire 2.5-mile trail is within the shrine, so we would have plenty of time to admire the scenery on our way to the top.

Once we set our feet to the trail, the looming *toriis* gave the impression of wandering through an immense vermillion forest. What had been so festive by day now began to feel oppressive: a prison with bars twice the size of a man. The forest around us awakened with a feral energy, and our passage up the mountainside quickly became one of mottled darkness, punctuated only by the light cast by occasional paper lanterns.

That said, the journey's countless gates were as remarkable as they were plentiful. Although there are rumored to be well over 30,000 dotting the mountainside, the priesthood itself has long-since lost count. They range anywhere in size from a hand-span to that of a California redwood. However, by offering gates to each of the shrine's 2.7 million annual visitors, the shrine has altogether cheapened their sacred appeal. Thousands of smaller gates (which can be sponsored for as little as $100) are strewn about the mountainside with no regard for propriety. In many places, they lie around in haphazard stacks ten gates deep: unseen and unremembered testaments to a tourist's impulse purchase, rather than their intended purpose as thresholds to the realm of gods.

*What is this? A gateway-to-the-spirit-realm for ANTS?*

The mountain itself also presented the issue of wildlife: a consideration that I had grown unaccustomed to in Japan. The country as a whole is not known for the hostility of its predators—even in the boonies, where nature is the rule and civilization the exception, the only incidents are a handful of bear attacks per year. In the city, of course, animal attacks are virtually unheard of.

Even still, and even though Mt. Inari is practically in the center of the city, monkeys and wild boar abound. Signboards warn hikers that feral monkeys are mischievous at their best and violent at their worst, and a wild boar would just as soon maul a human when threatened as we would a sausage when famished.

These reminders were unnecessary, as we were content to stick firmly to the trail. While the worst of the day's heat had faded, the memory of it remained fresh in our minds, and we had no intention of veering from the path and its many vending machines.

We passed a few others who were adventurous enough to brave the sacred mountain at night, but the shrine complex was mostly deserted by the time we reached the first lookout point. Past the lookout, the gentle stream of hikers with whom we had traveled slowed to a trickle. By the halfway point, it had become a drip, and when we finally reached the summit, we did so in solitude.

There was little to distinguish the end of our journey from the journey itself. Perhaps the mountaintop had a few more shrines than the ascent, and these were each crowded by marginally more miniature gates, but we only truly knew that we had reached the top by the fact that we could no longer continue upward.

Our descent took us on a winding trail down the back of the mountain, occasionally crisscrossing residential streets. Once we reached the base, we were ready to retire for the night.

❧

On the sixth morning of our trip, we slept in—a much-needed indulgence after four days of nonstop action. We ate a deep-fried breakfast, courtesy of 7-Eleven, before setting out at a leisurely pace for Osaka: Japan's traditional economic hub. From Kyoto Station, the train ride took just under half an hour, and we arrived around noon. The previous night's rest had left us feeling so refreshed that even the sun's ceaseless malevolence felt like little more than a cheery backdrop to the morning's activities.

The first of these was a visit to Osaka Castle, which was close enough to be plainly visible from the station. Our short walk there took us through its imposing gates and into the castle's dusty courtyard. The face of the alabaster castle is undoubtedly impressive—adorned as it is in resplendent greens and golds—but we had hoped to see more of the interior than what little could be glimpsed from the courtyard. However, we were dismayed to discover a single-file line of similarly-intentioned tourists that stretched far beyond the castle grounds and into the distance. Worse, the castle's caretakers had lacked the foresight to provide a shelter of any sort for these poor souls, so they remained entirely exposed to the elements. We had no intention of standing in the sun for an hour just to enter a poorly-ventilated tinderbox, so we snapped a few quick pictures and moved on. After cooling our heels for a bit in the shade overlooking the castle moat, we set off in search of lunch.

My friend from Osaka had recommended we try *kushikatsu,* a local specialty akin to deep-fried shish kebabs—and there is no better place to find these savory skewers than Shinsekai. With a name meaning "New World," this historic neighborhood was Japan's attempt at emulating Western culture in the early 20th century. It was created in 1912, with its northern half based on

Paris and its southern half on New York. The area's iconic Tsūtenkaku Tower is, itself, based on the Eiffel Tower.

Understandably, after the war, this neighborhood that was modeled after two western metropoles fell into disuse and disrepair. A criminal element took root soon after, leading to a downturn in the neighborhood's reputation. Even after the decline of gang culture in the 1990s, Shinsekai has had difficulty breaking free of its sordid history. An influx of prostitutes and homeless has done little to repair its image in the years since. In fact, it remains one of the only theoretically unsafe areas in Japan. (Or so I've been told. My brothers and I had no trouble there.)

In recommending *kushikatsu*, my Osakan friend had used the word "*kuidaore*," which I was unfamiliar with. In preparation for my brothers' trip, I researched the concept in further detail. It turns out that *kuidaore* is a pillar of Osakan culture, meaning "to eat oneself into ruin." It is most strongly associated with the Dōtonbori entertainment district, but I would hazard that nowhere is its spirit so well embodied as at Yokozuna Shinsekai Honten. This self-styled sumo restaurant offers outrageous quantities of Japanese food at a reasonable price—for example, forty pieces of fried chicken for $10. My brothers and I were drawn into this establishment by the sheer size of the window displays and noticed with delight that several customers had similarly-sized dishes at their table. The hostess seated us near the center of the restaurant, and we began to peruse the menu.

After scant deliberation, we ordered two kilograms of *yakisoba*—fried noodles. Our excitement quickly turned to dismay as the server set it down at our table a few minutes later with an audible *thunk*.

"There's no way we can finish this," Patrick said, matter-of-factly. I had once seen him inhale a burrito the size of a Yorkshire terrier in under a minute, so his apprehension concerned me nearly as much as the noodles themselves.

But, never underestimate the appetite of four young men with something to prove. We polished them off in twenty minutes flat; a serving platter, damp with grease, served as the only indication that such a herculean mound had ever existed at all.

"So," Patrick said, suddenly chipper. "Dessert?" The success had clearly restored his faith in our abilities.

"Patrick," Connor replied, incredulous.

"Actually, Con," Joe chimed in, pointing at the menu, "I kinda want to try this."

We all looked at the object of his desire: "Vanilla pudding. Feeds ten."

"Guys, we can't…" Connor began. He trailed off in futility after seeing the hunger in our eyes. So, we then ordered enough vanilla pudding to nourish a fielded soccer team. We were already uncomfortably full from the noodles, as well as a brief stint at a *kushikatsu* restaurant earlier in the afternoon. From the second that the waiter returned, a wobbly mountain of gelatin in tow, we knew that we were doomed to fail. Patrick began giggling at the absurdity of our mistake, and we were unable to help ourselves from joining in. Our sudden outburst drew stares from nearby tables.

In case I have not yet made it abundantly clear, Japan is a land of great propriety that places the utmost importance on the convenience of others. This made it especially jarring when Joe, possessed by some sudden alien urge, reached out and smacked the side of the pudding with the back of a large serving spoon, producing an audible *thwack* that cut through the murmurous din of the busy restaurant. Despite (and largely because of) its impropriety, the four of us spiraled into fits of muffled laughter from which there was no recovery. We barely held ourselves together long enough to choke down an impressive two-thirds of the dessert, pay our bill, and beat a hasty retreat.

It was late afternoon by the time we stepped back outside. Stomachs full twice over, our only remaining stop for the evening was Dōtonbori: Osaka's premier entertainment district. We made our way there on foot, pausing briefly at Namba Yasaka, a shrine in central Osaka with a unique lion's head design. From the shrine, a short 15-minute walk took us into Dōtonbori proper.

Dōtonbori, which refers to both the district at large and the canal cutting through its heart, is often considered Osaka's cultural center. In many ways, it is the Osakan equivalent of Times Square; flashy billboards, loud music, and the scent of frying seafood abound. It has the feel of an area both centuries-old and decades-new.

The canal can be traced back to its inception in 1612, when a local entrepreneur named Yasui Dōton leveraged his considerable wealth to expand the local Umezu River. Commerce had been slacking in recent years, but Yasui envisioned a grand canal connecting the two branches of the Yokobori trade river. Unfortunately, he met an untimely demise in 1615, during the Siege of Osaka, giving his life to protect Toyotomi Hideyori (who proceeded to take his own life shortly thereafter). Thankfully, the newly-appointed Lord of Osaka allowed Yasui's cousins to complete the project, and they named it Dōtonbori (Dōton Canal) in his honor.

The canal saw some use as a trade route during the next half-decade. However, it truly hit its stride in 1621, when the Tokugawa Shogunate designated the area along its banks as the city's official entertainment district. As *kabuki*—perhaps the most well-known form of Japanese theater—had gotten its start only two decades earlier, it had all the makings of a perfect storm. A thespian renaissance blossomed along the grassy shores of Dōton's canal, breathing true life into the district. By the 1660s, it was home to at least a dozen theaters, plus a handful of bars and restaurants built to accommodate the sudden flood of entertainment seekers.

Dōtonbori continued to flourish for many centuries, further reveling in the artistic revolution of the Edo Era. This prosperity lasted until the turn of the 19th century, when a waning interest in traditional theater saw the area's popularity lessen. The decline of Dōtonbori as a theater district was completed in February 1945, when its five remaining theaters were destroyed during the Allied bombing of Osaka. However, its legacy remained, and a postwar economic boom restored this once-bustling neighborhood into what it is today: a neon testament to man's ever-growing need for recreation.

My brothers and I reached Dōtonbori shortly before sunset. We visited the local sights that had made it onto my friend's shortlist of recommendations: the Kani Doraku crab, Kuidaore Taro, and the Glico running man billboard. As we visited these landmarks and others, we realized that Dōtonbori is absolutely rife with characters. The most famous shops all sport distinctive animatronic mascots which have, to some extent, become emblematic of the district as a whole. Newer establishments that have cropped up within the area have sought to emulate this retro charm, with more recent additions to the cast including a demonic cow and a walleyed dragon.

Although my brothers and I were quite certain that we would never be hungry again after eating at the sumo restaurant, the salty food and daytime sightseeing had left us feeling parched. We ducked into a nearby *izakaya* around sunset to escape the lingering heat and quench our thirst. Night had fallen in truth by the time we left the bar, tipsy but feeling refreshed.

While the entertainment district had been colorful by day, it was positively luminous at night, lit from above in a blinding neon haze. We wandered slowly through the crowded streets, tempted to further stuff our stomachs at one of the many local *takoyaki* joints. As this would have more or less killed us, however, cooler heads prevailed. We returned to Kyoto and our mountainside hotel.

## The Eastern Capital

That was it for Kansai Prefecture. The next morning, we checked out of our *ryokan*, bright and early, and boarded a series of trains bound for Tokyo. As this took my brothers and me back past Nagoya twice over, it was both exorbitantly expensive and somewhat exhausting. I spent the train ride in a blissful continuation of the previous night's sleep and soon awoke in the nation's capital.

We disembarked from the bullet train, still feeling a bit groggy. As we were making our way out of the station, Joe suddenly snorted, turning his head back the way we'd come.

"That was odd," he said.

Patrick, Connor, and I turned, but we didn't notice anything out of the ordinary.

"What's up?" I asked.

"We just walked by a toddler wearing a 'Fuck the War' shirt," he replied, pointing. We followed his gaze, and noticed a youngster of no more than two years old, skipping merrily alongside his parents with the pinnacle of English vulgarity emblazoned across his back.

That was not to be the only unfortunate mistranslation that we saw in Tokyo. In our remaining days in the nation's capital, we saw shirts reading "Skysc raper," "Until the tears runinto yournouth," and the distressingly vague "Sucky Sucky."

As an aside, it's interesting to see how the cultural connotation of some clothing brands has not survived the journey overseas. Playboy, for example, is a household brand that can be found on all manner of clothing and accessories. Among my students, I had high-schoolers with Playboy backpacks, a middle-aged woman with a Playboy clutch, and one adorable preschooler with the iconic bunny embroidered onto her hairband. Similarly, classically insecure middle-school girls would show up to my class sporting hot-pink Crocs, unaware that they were wearing the traditional uniform of a heavy-set dad on a riding mower. This may not be quite on par with Americans getting the Japanese instructions for instant-mac tattooed onto their bicep, thinking that it means "Courage," but it's amusing nonetheless.

Well, back to the station.

Truth be told, my previous visits to Tokyo had been a bit underwhelming. It is certainly an enormous, vibrant city, perpetually charged with a febrile energy, but no more so than New York or Chicago. Contrary to what I had been led to believe by the highly-romanticized depictions of anime, the nation's capital is, by and large, commercial.

Or, at least, that was my impression during previous visits. With my brothers by my side, however, it was bound to be a different story. As four young men, we were able to appreciate the city in a light that I simply couldn't with my parents present.

Our first night in the city was spent in Roppongi, a prominent night-life district. We killed a few hours at a crowded *izakaya* before returning to our B&B.

The next day saw us engaged in a whirlwind tour of the Tokyo tourist classics. Shibuya Crossing, Sensoji, Ueno Park—we left no stone unturned on the capital's most well-traveled path. My brothers had finally given in to the sun, and, without their thrice-daily showers, our pace increased exponentially. We managed to reach the last stop on our self-guided tour, Meiji Jingū, just before sunset. Like me, my brothers were most enamored by the religious sites; Meiji, in particular—shaded and serene—was their favorite.

*Of the 1,000 daily prayers at Meiji Jingū…*

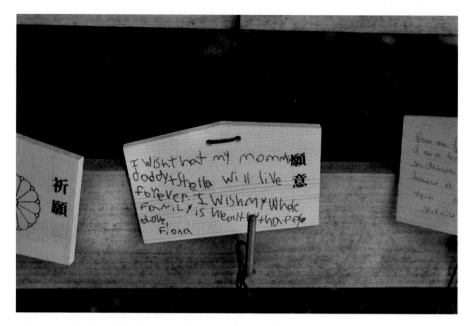

*...this was by far the most adorable*

For the evening, we had secured tickets to a baseball game at the nearby Meiji Jingu Stadium. The game featured the Yakult Swallows versus Nagoya's home team, the Chunichi Dragons. I had been to several previous Dragons games with an adult student as generous as he was fanatical, and I couldn't wait to share the experience with my siblings.

Unfortunately, my student had been both a season ticket-holder and a man of means. My brothers and I barely qualified as regular ticket-holders and were median men at best. Our seats, far off into left field, were anything but glamorous.

Have you ever returned to a playground that you once frequented as a child and tried to use the equipment, only to marvel at the fact that you ever fit there at all? That's what it felt like, trying to cram our considerable backsides into the economy seats. The four of us took to staggering our seating positions, two hunched forward and two with our backs flush against the seats, to avoid three hours of nonstop shoulder contact.

Having grown up in a less-than-illustrious era of Detroit sporting, I had to come to expect very little in the way of professional sports. The first year that I paid any real attention to professional football was the year that the Lions infamously went 0-16, a failure so resounding as to have only been matched once in NFL history (although, sadly, this was not the Lions' only winless season). Following that season-long shutout came the middling years of Detroit baseball. Once a year, my brothers and I would treat our dad to a game for Father's Day. I would inevitably doze off at these annual excursions into the world of baseball, lulled to sleep by the lethargic murmur of the listless crowd.

However, as I had learned from my previous Dragons games, Japanese baseball is a different beast entirely. It's one of the few remaining avenues for otherwise repressed Japanese businessmen to cut loose—other than drinking themselves into oblivion—and they do so with remarkable aplomb. Long before we took our seats, nearly an hour before the game began, both teams had already started competing chants intended to pump up their own team and (politely) rattle their opponents.

Eventually, when the call went out to hit the game's opening pitch, it was met by the King of Monsters himself. A man dressed as Godzilla waddled into the batter's box, took his position, and swung at the ball. He missed by a mile—encumbered as he was by a solid inch of sweaty rubber on all sides—but he may as well have been hammering the final nail into the coffin of Japanese stereotypes for all that it mattered to the crowd. Fans on either side of the pitch erupted in applause as he roared in frustration, threw down the bat, and waddled back off of the diamond.

Then the game began in truth, and the cheers became one-sided. Unlike Western sports, where fans delight in distracting their opponents, Japanese fans remain respectfully quiet when the other team is at bat. Shortly after the game began, I flagged down a stewardess and ordered four beers. After a while, these eased our discomfort, so we relaxed and sat back to enjoy the game.

Now, as I mentioned, I have never been the most diehard fan of professional baseball. But, in Japan, I was a Dragons fan—and an ardent one at that. My brothers, lacking any prior knowledge of either

*Just a day in the life*

team, started off cheering for the Dragons as well. Sometime in the bottom of the fifth inning, however, Joe began to join in the opposing team's rallying cry: "Go, Go Swallows!" Patrick soon joined him, seduced by the allure of an English chant. With our group of four split down the middle, we became much more engaged in the game. Connor and I redoubled the enthusiasm of our support to drown out the traitors in our midst, and the remaining innings were spent cheering with—and jeering at—one another, displaying none of our neighbors' cordial restraint.

The game ended in a rout, with the Dragons claiming a decisive victory. The four of us left the stadium with Connor and me basking in our vicarious glory.

Our next stop was the Golden Gai district in Shinjuku. Having previously only heard the phrase "Golden Gai" spoken aloud, I had envisioned a luminous display of bronzed Adonises. Thus, I was sorely disappointed to discover that it was little more than a dingy collection of small bars, some of which had rooms so cramped as to be accessible only on all fours. We were invited into one such cranny by a boisterous Scottish barkeep, but we declined after being informed that the air conditioning had given out weeks ago, and the room could now double as a wood stove in a pinch.

We ducked into several crowded bars before finding one with adequate seating. This was apparently because they had economized all of the space from their stairwell into the bar itself, resulting in a low ceiling that had clearly tested the mettle of many a drunken foreigner's skull. We enjoyed our last night in Tokyo in the relative comfort of the cozy bar, playing cards and chatting with some bilingual locals.

The following morning, we said our goodbyes to the nation's capital and returned to Nagoya for one last day. Much of it was spent preparing for my brothers' ultimate departure back to America, but we still found the time to return to Sakae for one last bowl of Ichiran ramen.

As my brothers and I exited the metro station downtown, we noticed that the street was closed off a few blocks further down. We headed in that direction and stumbled (quite literally) into the midst of the Nagoya

*Patrick narrowly avoids disaster*

Summer Festival, which had, unbeknownst to us, been taking place that weekend. We bailed on Ichiran, opting instead for one last batch of fried festival food.

This particular festival saw residents from nearby towns come to showcase their hometown's talent in the big city, with acts ranging anywhere from *shamisen* quartets to interpretive dance. While we were marveling at one such performance from a nearby fishing village, Patrick commented that we had managed to accidentally find a startling number of festivals. I responded that this must have been because of the sheer number of festivals available and popped open my phone to confirm this statement. In doing so, I discovered that no less than three other festivals were going on within the city at that very moment.

All in all, it was an appropriate send-off for my brothers on their last night in Japan. We drank, we watched the performances, and when we finally returned to my cramped apartment, we did so with a sense of contentedness. Of course, I was sad to see them off at the airport the following morning, but I truly felt as if I'd gotten the chance to show them what my new life was all about. We'd seen and done so many things during their short stay that, at the end of the day, I was just thankful for the amazing opportunity we'd had.

# Setomono Festival

In the months leading up to September, my students had told me tales of the wondrous Setomono Festival, which would transform Seto from a sleepy country backwater into a bustling center of fictile commerce. Having previously been to a few smaller festivals within the city, which were underwhelming at best despite having been similarly anticipated, I was not overly inclined to believe them.

However, as the months passed and the festival date drew nearer, I began to question my disbelief. Several weeks before the festival, promotional fliers began appearing around town, first in trickles, then in droves. By the time September arrived, once-destitute pottery shops were undergoing heavy renovations, and the larger stores were expanding their inventories.

As with most work-related things, this registered as a sense of mild interest before any forming opinion was swept away by the tide of day-to-day minutiae. Per the insightful direction of our esteemed manager, however, it was decided several weeks in advance that we would all attend work the day of the festival wearing *yukatas*—the traditional Japanese leisure garment that I had worn twice before at the mountainside hotel in Kyoto. With this addition of a way that the festival would affect me personally, my interest was finally piqued.

About one week before the festival's scheduled date, a fleet of white vans appeared outside of the building where I taught. (Parti Seto was one of the town's main cultural centers, situated next to the only train station and a festival-ready public square.) As an American, I had come to view construction details as nothing more than a taxpayer-incensing waste of manpower. In Japan, of course, there was no such waste. Through the concerted effort of a dozen laborers, the bus stop behind our building was transformed into a workable festival ground in just a few days. Excited, I made an appointment to rent my *yukata* on the morning of the event.

Unfortunately, I found out quite late the night before that we would have to report to work an hour earlier than expected for assistance in donning our *yukatas*. So, I arrived in Seto, dark-eyed and droopy-tailed, more or less alongside the sun. I wore my most breathable outfit—gym shorts and a graphic tee—which made running into several students on the way to the kimono store all the more uncomfortable.

The shopkeeper arrived shortly after I did and led me into the back room to change. As she spoke very little English, and my Japanese vocabulary did not yet include "useful terms when instructing strangers to disrobe," this was accomplished through a great deal of gesturing and nervous laughter on her part. The whole affair took perhaps ten minutes, but the result was, to the *yukata's* credit, quite striking. Gone was the gym rat of moments prior; Festival Kyle had arrived.

My co-workers, Fumika, Felicity, and Rina, trickled in shortly afterward. Putting on their robes proved a lengthier process, which involved a lot of hemming and hawing (pun fully intended) on the part of the seamstress. But, eventually, they too were spectacularly enrobed, and we went outside to enjoy the festival for a few moments.

(Fumika and I would begin dating one week after this festival. I like to think that I have the *yukata* to thank for this sudden development.)

Enjoying the festival before work turned out to be a terribly demotivating decision. Between the sizzling food stalls, the primal background drumbeat, and the vast array of beautiful pottery on sale, just about the last thing that I wanted to do afterward was stand in a stuffy room for several hours.

But, stand stuffily I did. Many of my students were also wearing *yukatas* or various other forms of traditional dress, which helped to lighten the mood inside. The morning passed by quickly and without incident. By the time lunch arrived, my stomach was grumbling something fierce for the many fried, chocolate-covered, or otherwise decadent foods that were visible from my classroom window.

For lunch, we got the festival classics: *yakisoba, takoyaki,* and cheese dogs, each of which was freshly cooked and, accordingly, the temperature of the sun. The weather had only slightly begun to cool from the hellish nightmare of Obon, so the four of us attempted to find a patch of shade in which to eat.

Approximately 3,000 other people had had the same idea, so we ended up perched on a curb in the blazing sun.

When the seamstress had helped me put on the *yukata* that morning, she had first gestured for me to remove my shirt, which I did. She had then indicated that I should do the same with my shorts, but I politely declined. This proved to be a wise decision indeed, as the curb on which we sat was just low enough to put my knees level with my shoulders, leaving my *yukata* draped open in a "come hither" pose that left very little to the imagination. Several passing students approached us for pictures while we ate, so I was immensely glad to have shorts on underneath. I wasn't yet sure how I planned to leave Japan, but "deported for indecent exposure" was not high on the list.

Speaking of indecency, about an hour after lunch, the *yukata's* cultural allure began to be overrun by the much more imminent, biological need to use the restroom. Considering it had taken ten minutes and several belts to strap me into the damn thing to begin with, this proved to be no easy feat. After some experimentation with positioning, which included both the deep lunge and the unsupported handstand, I finally managed to find relief. Any other building staff unfortunate enough to find themselves peering beneath the bathroom door to identify the cursing American must have been quite alarmed to alternatively see two, four, and zero limbs in contact with the floor at any given moment.

The *yukata* never quite fit right again after that. Once the belts loosened, it was held up only by constant adjustments and sheer force of will. The unyielding wooden sandals that it had come with also began to wear on my nerves. Altogether, the outfit managed to simulate the discomfort of walking on a hardwood floor while simultaneously preventing bodily expulsions of any kind—except perspiration, which it engendered in ceaseless waves throughout the day.

Once our classes finished for the evening, the staff all hurried to close the school. Then, Felicity, Fumika, Rina, and I stepped outside into the thrumming energy of the cool night air.

By this point, I considered myself something of a seasoned festival veteran. I had been to so many that the memories of each seemed to blend together into one long stream of fried chicken and *taiko* drums. There's a magical quality to these festivals; children run around shrieking in masks, music abounds, and the alcohol flows freely enough to make you forget about the cares of the outside world.

For me, the Setomono festival didn't feel magical. Instead, it felt like a great many people with the vague familiarity of previous passersby, in a town that I had become intimately familiar with, having the time of their lives.

We grabbed some beer from a nearby concession stand and began to wind our way through the tightly-packed streets. While the Setomono festival is a celebration of the year elapsed, as well as a celebration of hope for the year to come, it's also an invaluable opportunity for the city's many local artists to display and sell their works. The streets were lined with dozens of ceramic stalls on either side, and even the most rambunctious festivalgoers stopped by to carefully appreciate the beauty and intricacies at each. The four of us wandered the streets for an hour or so, laughing and drinking. We passed a few teenage students that were sipping surreptitiously from unmarked cans, but we just greeted them politely and continued on our way.

As the festival drew to a close, a fireworks show began in the street outside of my school. It was unable to match the sheer scale and ferocity of American pyrotechnics, but it was a perfectly exciting end to a long day. (As an aside, my Japanese co-workers referred to each of the show's many highlights as "climaxes," which amused Felicity and me to no end.)

Following the fireworks, we had some time to spare before leaving Seto. The crowd was still outrageous, and we didn't fancy the thought of packing our sweaty selves onto a crowded train just to go drink elsewhere. So, like any reasonable teachers, we loaded up on cheap booze at the nearest convenience store and returned to our school. The baby classroom was the only one not in full view of the building's security cameras, so the four of us sat cross-legged among puppets and wood blocks, sipping our beverages and watching the teeming masses below. Felicity tossed on her Spotify, and madness ensued.

As I mentioned in her introduction, Fumika has long since had a fondness for all things Latin—particularly music. So, when Felicity's Spotify started to play a certain Spanglish ballad from Canada's favorite tattooed dreamboat, all hell broke loose. The girls began to dance, creating a backlit spectacle for the uncaring masses below. I suggested we turn off the lights, but that undoubtedly only made it stranger for anyone who happened to glance casually upwards: the entire teaching staff, and manager to boot, slowly gyrating in the darkened window of the baby classroom.

When I was younger, I believed that my teachers slept at school. I can't imagine what any of our students who witnessed such a spectacle must now believe.

Several songs later, I felt the need to answer the call of nature once more, which involved a lengthy walk to the nearest staff restroom. By that point, I was truly fed up with *yukata's* wooden footwear, whose curved bottoms made balancing difficult even at peak sobriety. As I was rushing headlong toward the deepest valley thereof, they were damn near impossible to walk in. I cast them aside without a second thought and never looked back. (Okay, fine. I gingerly placed them into my cushioned backpack to return in perfect condition the following week. Are you happy now, fun police?)

After my business was complete, I returned to the classroom and my frolicking friends within. We celebrated a short while longer as the crowds dispersed below. Once they had sufficiently thinned, we locked up the school once more, stumbled into line with the rest of the drunken stragglers, and boarded the train out of Seto.

# Okinawa

After that, time passed as it is so wont to do. September came and went, as did several friends, but their visits were but blips of excitement on an otherwise unbroken canvas of mundanity. In early Autumn, however, my overworked co-workers and I booked a much-needed tropical getaway to Okinawa. Since this required the four of us to book flights and hotels several weeks in advance, I had the opportunity for once to research our destination for more than a few hurried moments pre-departure. Much of what I found surprised me, but nothing so much as just how removed Okinawa is from the rest of Japan, both geographically and culturally.

This stems from many factors, not the least of which is distance. Okinawa lies on the outskirts of the East China Sea, nearly 650 kilometers from mainland Japan (approximately twice the distance from London to Paris). In truth, it is closer to Taiwan than it is to Japan, and it only officially joined the nation in the late 19th century. For four and a half centuries prior, Okinawa was known as the Ryukyu Kingdom: an independent island nation with its own language, religion, and history. It played a critical role in the Southeast Asian maritime trade, which resulted in its invasion and subjugation by Japan in the early 1600s. However, it was allowed to remain an autonomous vassal state until it was formally annexed in 1872.

Japan's Meiji-era government, notoriously implacable in its pursuit of modernization, attempted to eliminate every trace of Ryukyu culture shortly after its annexation. This injustice, combined with seething post-war animosity following the Battle of Okinawa (which saw nearly a quarter of the civilian population killed), reportedly left many Okinawan locals with a lingering resentment toward both foreigners and central Japan itself.

Of course, to speak of the forest ignores the trees. None of this conflict or history was apparent to Felicity or me as we stepped off our plane into Japanese paradise. In fact, the locals seemed even more amiable than Japanese mainlanders, who are already considerably so. We breezed right through security—you don't need to show identification of any kind for domestic flights within Japan—and chartered a ride to our villa with a portly old taxi driver named Shun.

By this point, my Japanese was fluent enough for small talk, but Shun spoke an Okinawan dialect that I had trouble understanding. I let him know as much within the first few minutes of the ride, but he was not so easily deterred. Shun talked nonstop for nearly forty minutes, all of which was met with uneasy smiles and tentative nods on our part. He seemed content with our noncommittal responses until we neared our destination. There, he repeated the same question several times, then pulled the taxi over—meter still running, of course—and fumbled around with Google translate for a while. Eventually, we pieced together that he was trying to sell us an expensive handwritten guidebook of the area, exactly 0% of which was in English, so we politely declined. He deposited us at our villa a few minutes later, robbed of several minutes' taxi fare and lifespan.

We had selected this particular lodging solely because the listing had touted both a hot tub and billiards, or "pool and pool," which tickled our fancy immensely. While this is the sort of reasoning from which all good decisions arise, it left us with little confidence to fall back on when Shun dropped us off at a corrugated steel shanty. We were greeted at the door by Homma-san, the villa's proprietor and (we would soon learn) Japanese grandpa extraordinaire. After a series of bewildering introductions, wherein he claimed that he and his two cats were blood relatives, Homma-san led us away from his home and over to a separate complex. He showed us through an unassuming gate in an unimpressive wall, directly into paradise.

Homma-san's villa exceeded our wildest expectations. It did indeed have the aforementioned pool and pool, as well as a dart machine, two fully-stocked private bars, an industrial-grade kitchen, and a detached bedroom complete with a fully-retractable wall overlooking a bluff toward the ocean.

We explored the villa for a while, then made our way to the roof. It had a small, weather-worn table and what I can only describe as a suicide swing:

a slippery wooden board attached by two rusted chains to a rickety frame, overlooking a 40-foot drop into certain death below. I regarded it warily, but we were far too sober to test our luck just yet.

Homma-san asked us if we were hungry, to which we replied that we weren't. With a dismissive wave of his hand, he showed us to yet another bar and began cutting vegetables. In truth, Felicity and I wanted nothing more than to shed our stuffy outfits and seek the buoyant embrace of tropical waters, but we didn't want to offend our host by rejecting his kind offer. So, we sat as he prepared us one small dish, then another, and another.

In total, he prepared us a six-course meal over the course of forty minutes. This involved significantly more clambering than any meal preparation has the right to, as Homma-san would be dutifully attending to the stove one moment, rummaging through assorted shelves the next, then standing on the countertop banging on the side of his TV moments later.

He plied us with deceptively sweet drinks while we ate, sending our ability to speak Japanese and our confidence that we could do so rocketing in different directions. We soon realized that he was deaf, which explained the earlier confusion about his cats' lineage. With the aid of Google Translate, however, we were able to have something closely resembling a conversation. Homma-san watched soccer on TV while we spoke, occasionally emitting an embittered "*Yabai!*"—the quintessential expression of an aged man's displeasure.

As Felicity and I finished our final course, Homma-san replaced his cooking utensils with cutlery and settled in to watch the game from behind the bar. We thanked him profusely for the meal and retreated to the game room.

Now, as I've previously mentioned, Felicity was not the strongest drinker that I'd ever known. However, having come to Japan straight out of college, she was among the most willing. She had sucked down four or five fruity drinks during Homma-san's extravagant lunch and was, therefore, no competition as we played billiards, then darts. Felicity responded to this bevy of losses by increasing her alcohol consumption tenfold, which quickly reduced her to a gibbering pile of drunken defeat.

Several hours later, Rina and Fumika arrived at the villa. Homma-san greeted them at the front gate, then gave them the same tour he had given us. They were more or less famished on arrival, having caught a later and longer flight than us. That also happened to be the night of Japan versus South Africa in the Rugby World Cup—a nerve-wracking clash occurring in Tokyo. Homma-san ushered us back to the bar from earlier and poured us three beers.

(He strategically failed to provide a fourth for young Felicity, hinting at a keen observance behind his weathered eyes.) He cooked us another decadent meal while we tried (and failed) to comprehend the intricacies of rugby.

Half an hour into the dinner, a hairless Caucasian man in a state of partial undress emerged from a previously unseen side door and took his place at Homma-san's side. This shirtless stranger introduced himself as Benny and asked if he could join us at the bar. What started off as a rather tepid conversation quickly developed into one of the most bizarre encounters of my young life.

We made the basic inquiries expected of any foreigners meeting abroad: "Where are you from? How long have you been here? Have you ever been involuntarily celibate for a period exceeding three years?"

Oh, no, wait. We didn't ask that last one, because it would be an absolutely ludicrous thing to discuss with strangers.

Don't worry. We'll get there.

When prompted, Benny informed us that, in addition to being an English teacher, he helped Homma-san out part-time at another site. They had the sort of chemistry that can only be found between the relentlessly talkative and the comfortably deaf and were, overall, unbearably wholesome.

Benny was an Englishman who had arrived in Japan nearly a decade ago with his now-estranged wife, a fact that would soon be expanded upon in lurid detail. He had been living in Okinawa for the past three years, however, and seemed impressively knowledgeable about the island and its secrets. Benny shared a few of these with our party, but he spent most of the next half hour watching the rugby game in amiable silence. Eventually, he excused himself and returned to the hidden room from whence he had come.

Fumika, Felicity, and Rina returned to the main villa a short while later. This left me alone with a partially deaf, aggressively monolingual gentleman with no apparent interest in conversing, so I excused myself and left the bar. For lack of anything else to do, I decided to check on Benny in his secret room. It turned out to be a private movie theater/karaoke room, whose soundproof walls made me 82% more concerned that I would soon be little more than a series of headlines and a membranous jacket.

Benny was using Netflix, which is to say flipping through hundreds of viable options while lamenting the lack of choices. We started chatting idly about what led us to Japan, which is where things went horribly awry. My reason was simple, if a bit uninspired: boredom and wanderlust. Benny's was—by comparison or otherwise—batshit crazy.

Benny first met his wife in India while on a nondenominational mission trip to the Punjab region. He initially expressed no interest in her whatsoever, which she responded to by stalking him for a period of several years. He fled from country to country, relentlessly pursued by a madwoman from abroad.

"Then," he added matter-of-factly, as if it was the only logical conclusion, "I figured it was about time we shacked up together." And so they did. By this point, their chase had returned them to India, but Benny planned to depart soon for a teaching opportunity in Japan. His then-fiancée, conveniently a Japanese native, decided to follow him one last time.

Except, that's too simple an end for young Benny's story. On a weekend trip back to India, several years later, his wife got caught up with the Hare Krishnas. Benny, by merit of marital persuasion, was compelled to do the same. As he explained it, the Hare Krishnas were a reasonable lot overall, but their tenets strictly prohibited sexual contact of any kind except for procreation. As he and his wife had already found time to pop out three children amidst the stalking and traveling, their sex life ended on that day.

Now, I understand that this information isn't something that you particularly want to hear. It's jarring, graphic, and far too personal. To be fair, it wasn't quite what I, a drunken foreigner locked in a soundproof room with a shirtless madman, hoped to be discussing either.

So, back to Benny. Then ensued what he called "The Dark Ages," where they remained married and celibate for three more years. Suffice to say, this was not Benny's preference. I was inclined to believe him from the get-go, but in case I harbored any lingering desire to join the Hairless Hindis, he proceeded to elaborate in torrid detail about the physical and psychological dangers of prolonged abstinence.

"At one point, I was literally going crazy," he explained. "I felt like my body was on fire all the time, and I couldn't think straight. Once everything backs up, it all just goes to your brain, ya know?"

I likely responded to this flood of personal information with something along the lines of "I'm Kyle, by the way."

Just as my acutely unnoticed discomfort reached a fever pitch, the airy tinkle of inebriated laugher signaled the return of my fairer friends. I excused myself with a hastily constructed, "Damn, that's crazy man. Well, I don't want to keep you," and rejoined my friends at the bar.

From there, my recollection of the night gets rather hazy. We laughed, we drank, and—as one vividly frigid memory would suggest—we took a midnight dip in the unheated pool. Specifics aside, we enjoyed several hours of uninterrupted revelry before finally wandering off to bed.

Speaking of beds, I had claimed one in the room with a retractable wall by merit of having placed my bags there first. Therefore, I awoke the next morning, fuzzy-headed and foggy-eyed, to the most beautiful of sights: a tranquil ocean, radiantly lit by the first few rays of an Okinawan sunrise. Better yet, I got to enjoy it from the boundless comfort of a proper bed—something that my company-provided apartment conspicuously lacked.

The sunrise seen from atop Mt. Fuji had been breathtakingly magnificent; from beneath layers of enveloping sheets, it was simply divine. I lay in bed watching the sun and waves for the better part of an hour, until hunger began to outweigh my island indolence. I ate a quick breakfast, courtesy of my friends in the main house, then drifted into the pool for a lazy start to our morning activities.

In the early afternoon, Fumika and Felicity expressed a vague interest in exploring the island. Homma-san's otherwise-defunct ears perked up at this, and he offered us his service as a tour guide. We took him up on his generous offer.

Homma-san's car was a Mitsubishi Pajero: a hulking beast reminiscent of a mid-90s Humvee. It made easy work of the rocky, uneven terrain as we traversed through tangled mangroves and overgrown cemeteries. A few minutes later, we arrived at a collection of hammocks and trailers overlooking a cliff toward the ocean.

Moments after we arrived, Benny emerged from a nearby grove of trees, as shirtless and exuberant as ever. He greeted us casually, as if I hadn't been drowning in the totality of his life's regrets only the evening before, and introduced the collection of shanties as their next property. It was quite charming, if a bit rustic, and the view overlooking the bay area was delightful.

We whiled away the morning smacking golf balls into the jungle below, only occasionally met with yelps of bewildered pain from below. Around noon, Homma-san relinquished the keys to his car and suggested that we go forth with it. So it was that dear, diminutive Rina, the only one among us with a Japanese driver's license, found herself dwarfed behind the wheel of his hulking Pajero.

Our first stop (once we determined how Rina could peer over the dashboard without straining her neck) was Chinen Park: a lovely little mesa overlooking the sea. The sun was shining, the breeze was heavenly, and we were just within earshot of the waves crashing far below.

As with any breathtaking natural wonder, its beauty was marred by a garish man-made gift shop.

In addition to the usual assortment of cheap knickknacks to misplace one day and never again consider, this shop offered seaweed ice cream—a gastronomical peculiarity, even by Japan's notoriously adventurous standards. By that point, I was willing to subject myself to just about anything that promised a unique experience, so I promptly ordered two scoops.

It tasted exactly unlike I expected it to, in that it was actually quite palatable. It was as if someone had looked at a perfect scoop of creamy vanilla and thought, "Hmm. This could use some slimy grass."

We continued sightseeing for an hour or so before returning to the villa, weary and sunburnt. After a brief poolside nap, we asked Homma-san about local snorkeling opportunities. He grunted noncommittally, piled a mountain of equipment into the back of his car, and climbed into the driver's seat. We followed suit, and he drove us to the beach.

Now, to be clear, when I say that Homma-san drove us to the beach, I don't mean that he dropped us off at a parking lot within convenient walking distance. I mean that he drove us through that parking lot, across a perilously narrow outcropping that extended no further than two centimeters from the sides of the car in either direction, and directly onto the rocky beach. It was a thrilling experience that could have just as easily sent us tumbling into the murky depths below.

Homma-san parked close to the water, retrieved a lawn chair from his trunk, and fell into a deep sleep. While he rested, we enjoyed some fried chicken by the water's edge before snorkeling as we'd intended.

The reef was spectacular. It was brilliant, full of life, and easily accessible from the shore. It also helped me realize just how much I had missed swimming after ten months inland. The weightlessness, the freedom to move in any direction—I could have drifted there for hours had the clouds not rolled in.

Alas, they did, and we followed suit. We roused Homma-san from his reverie, and graciously allowed him to ferry us back to our palatial villa.

He treated us to one last delicious island meal. We thanked him profusely, then retired to the roof with a bottle of sake to marvel at the stars and—as the conversation took a bizarre twist—exchange ghost stories.

Surprisingly, there are many similarities between Japanese and American stories; women in mirrors and hook-handed vagabonds make appearances in both. However, Fumika and Rina also shared a couple of stories that were well and truly Japanese. One such story was that of the *Kuchisake-onna*, or the Slit-Mouthed Woman.

As one might surmise from her ghoulish name, *Kuchisake-onna's* mouth is slit wide open from ear to ear. There are several explanations as to how she came to acquire this disfigurement. In some versions of the story, it was a romantic rival, jealous of her beauty. In others, a medical procedure gone horribly awry. Or perhaps she received the wound as punishment for infidelity against her husband, a powerful samurai. In any case, all iterations of her story include her untimely death with a general distaste for menfolk.

After her death, she returned as an *onryō*, or malicious spirit, bearing the same disfigurement. But, not to worry—this is Japan, land of the unabashed germaphobe. She simply wears a surgical mask to cover her face, blending right in, and goes about her day. Unfortunately, she will occasionally approach a random man and ask, "Am I beautiful?"

Now, maybe this poor fellow is having a bad day. It could be cold, or rainy, or perhaps he's just an honorable man in a happily-committed relationship. But if, for whatever reason, he replies, "No," the Slit-Mouthed Woman stabs him to death.

This part of the story was delivered so abruptly that I had to confirm that I had heard it correctly.

"She stabs him?"

"Yes."

"With what?"

"A knife."

"Why does she have a knife?"

"To stab people."

Moving on, then.

But maybe the man is feeling a bit frisky, and he quite likes that this otherwise unassuming stranger has approached him with apparent romantic intent. If he replies in the affirmative, the woman removes her mask, revealing her grotesque smile. She then repeats her question, albeit this time with a bit more spittle.

If the man replies, "No," well, you know the drill—death by stabbing. If he replies, "Yes," however, Kuchisake-onna will still attack him, carving his face to match her own. It's a classic "knife and a sharp face" scenario.

But, all hope is not lost for our randomly-selected hero. If he repeatedly describes her as average-looking (every woman's dream), she will get frustrated and leave. Or, as with any malevolent spirit, she can be easily distracted by money and hard candies. Giving her either will placate her long enough to escape.

So, what is the moral of the story of the Slit-Mouthed Woman? Basically, if a woman in a face mask ever approaches you and asks if she's beautiful, toss some candy at her and walk away. Disfigured ghoul women aside, validation-seeking questions like these are simply not the solid foundation upon which a healthy relationship is built. Plus, on the off chance that it was just a genuine pick-up attempt, who doesn't like candy to deal with rejection?

Eventually, the pleasant ocean breeze turned chilly, and the sake ran dry. Fumika and I returned downstairs to chat for a bit before heading to bed. At the bar, we were interrupted by our final encounter with Benny the British Barbarian.

Concerned with the number of beer cans in his immediate vicinity, we inquired as to how he would be returning to his trailer that night. He assured us that he would not be driving home; instead, he would be staying at another bungalow on the same property as our own. This did little to comfort us.

Benny explained that the second building was also available for rent, at a much cheaper rate, but enjoyed none of the same amenities as the main villa. He offered to give us a tour, which we agreed to after a long moment of consideration. On the one hand, I hadn't overly enjoyed my first close-quarters experience with Benny and didn't relish the idea of sharing a confined space with him once more. On the other hand, I am an avid proponent of traveling frugally whenever possible, and the deluxe villa had cost upwards of $1,000 for two nights. Fumika and I reluctantly followed him into the second house—we were pleasantly surprised to leave several minutes later with our skin and psyches still intact.

Just when I began thinking it would be my first wholly benign encounter with Benny, Fumika was startled by a large grasshopper that flew across her path. Benny gestured toward it casually and explained, "Don't worry about him. He's here to see me."

With an inward sigh of resignation, I gave an expectant, "Oh?"

Benny nodded affirmatively and continued. "Yeah, there used to be only one around here. He used to visit me at the bar every night, so I started talking to him. After a while, he brought his family, and now we're friends."

As Fumika and I didn't even attempt to conceal our disbelief, he hastily added, "I know it sounds crazy, but they really are intelligent creatures. When you talk to them, you can see the understanding in their eyes."

Ah, all settled, then.

We said our goodnights to Benny and headed off to bed. That is not where our tale ends, however. That night, Homma-san's poor little villa was rocked by a doozy of a sub-tropical typhoon.

It started as a drizzle, which soon worsened into a steady downpour. I reluctantly got out of bed to close the mechanically-retractable bedroom wall around 2:00 AM—this proved to be a fortuitous decision indeed, as not thirty minutes later, the howling wind and driving rain knocked the villa's power out. Preparing for a 6:00 AM flight in utter darkness with the wind whipping mercilessly through cracks in the wall was still an unpleasant experience, but it would have been much worse had we been unable to close the wall entirely.

But, prepare we did, and quickly. The four of us then waited for our taxi in the darkened silence of the main villa. By the time it finally arrived, we were ready to go anywhere that the lights functioned, and the walls didn't rattle quite so alarmingly with each gust of wind.

Homma-san ran out after us as we piled into the cab, apologizing profusely for the blackout. He gave one last herculean "*Yabai!*" at the absurdity of the situation before sending us on our way.

We arrived at Naha Airport with no trouble and wearily boarded our flight. A few hours later, we were back to Nagoya and business as usual.

So, how to describe Okinawa? It was an unforgettable Japanese experience, which was uniquely un-Japanese. Had it not been for the language we spoke, it could have just as easily been Hawaii or the Caribbean. That said, it truly didn't matter which country we were in. The locals were pleasant, the weather was gorgeous, and the wine flowed freely. My impression was undoubtedly painted a few shades brighter by the brilliance of Homma-san's villa, but Okinawa itself is a must-see for anyone who likes crystal-clear waters, the spirit of adventure, and genuinely kind-hearted people.

# Kiso River Valley

In November, Fumika and I took a trip to the Kiso River Valley. I had been there once before to hike a portion of the Nakasendo Trail (a preserved trade route of enormous importance during the Edo Period), and the two of us planned to do the same. The Japanese maples in Nagano were at their autumnal peak, and the changing leaves promised to provide a radiant backdrop to our excursion.

Fumika and I planned to hike from Magome to Tsumago: two of the sixty-nine post towns that grew and flourished along the trail during its centuries of use. Many of these towns fell into disuse and disrepair during the Meiji Era, as pedestrian trade routes were made obsolete by the construction of railroads. These two, however, as well as the stretch of trail between them, were recognized by the Japanese government as National Historic Sites in 1987, leading to their restoration and revival. Now, they serve as tourist attractions and monuments to the region's history.

We arrived in Magome in the early afternoon via public transport, eager to get moving.

Magome was a charming little hamlet, set into the rolling hills of the valley amongst rice paddies and not much else. It had a carefully cultivated rustic atmosphere, with buried power lines and little visible technology. Fumika and I were delighted to discover that even the vending machines were wood-paneled as a sort of agrarian camouflage.

We began with a leisurely stroll through the cobblestoned streets, stopping every so often to drop into the many tiny shops and eateries. Most of these sold *omiyage* boxes—edible souvenirs that travelers are expected to bring back

122

for their friends and family. Fumika and I enjoyed some local specialties as we shopped, such as *nureokaki*—moist rice cakes—and seasonal vegetable udon.

After an hour in Magome, we reached the end of the main shopping street that led directly onto the trail. The clear skies and cool breeze stirred our spirits, so we set off along the Nakasendo.

The trail is 4.7 miles long (7.6 km), winding through forests, along rivers, and atop ravines. Most of it is quite well-defined, but it can be difficult to keep your bearings in a few stretches. By the time we began walking, the sun was high in the sky, and we knew we would have to race against the clock to make it to Tsumago by sunset. Although Japan is an incredibly safe country overall, neither of us were particularly keen on the idea of spending the night huddled alone in the woods.

Our walk was pleasant, if uneventful. We were alone on the road to Tsumago, due in no small part to the fact that we had started a few hours later than recommended. This did little to dampen our spirits, though, as we ambled along beneath the brilliant sunset pastels of the mountain's maples. True to our expectations, they were at their most radiant.

*Kōyō*, or the season of changing leaves, is one of Japan's most popular sightseeing seasons, second only to *hanami*—the blooming of cherry blossoms in March. Unlike *hanami*, however, where there are a few particular places to enjoy the best and most bountiful views, practically the entire country is ripe for viewing during *kōyō*. The afternoon was an exercise in walking a dozen feet, marveling at a particular tree's colors, walking a bit farther, and repeating.

*Over the river and through the woods*

Perhaps twenty minutes into this cycle, I remarked to Fumika that we had passed a great many fuzzy white insects that I initially mistook for snow. She introduced them as *yukimushi*—literally, "snow bugs." They derived their name from their wintry appearance, as well as the fact they were traditionally held to foretell of a coming winter storm. That day was a balmy 54° Fahrenheit (12° C), immediately disproving that centuries-old belief, but the way they drifted lazily about on the autumn breeze did bear an uncanny resemblance to the first gentle powder of the season.

"Would you like to see one?" Fumika asked, reaching up to gently stroke one with the palm of her hand. When she brought it back in, I was surprised to see that the *yukimushi* had alit comfortably on the tip of her forefinger.

"They're very relaxed creatures," she explained. "We used to catch dozens of them when we were younger. If you hold them long enough, they'll leave their snow on you."

I reached up to test this theory and caught a delightfully fuzzy friend of my own. It was about the size of a gnat and remained where it had landed for several minutes. When it finally caught a gust of wind and fluttered off, it did indeed leave a light dusting of powder on my thumb.

This would not be our only encounter with woodland critters that day. We also came across several collections of foliar figures, freshly carved from the many broad, silver leaves that covered the path. These took many shapes, such as Tiki masks, people, and small rabbits, and would have been downright adorable had they not been fastened to the trailside by means of ocular impalation. These grotesque caricatures, combined with the sickeningly sweet aroma that occasionally drifted across the trail, had the two of us concerned that we would soon come upon a crook-nosed lady with an affinity for broomsticks and a glutinous cottage.

Throughout the afternoon, we also noticed several bear bells dotting the trail at irregular intervals. These large copper bells allow hikers to announce their presence to any nearby predators in the hope of avoiding unwanted surprises. At first, I paid them little mind; however, as we ventured deeper into the woods, and they began appearing more frequently, I started to ring them with increasing vigor.

"You know, you don't have to do that so hard *every* time," Fumika remarked, after one particularly enthusiastic ringing.

I responded that an expert's decision to make bear deterrents more readily available is, in fact, the only grounds that one needs to utilize said deterrents as liberally and emphatically as possible. She saw the wisdom of my ways, and we spent the rest of the afternoon wailing on every bell that we passed, no doubt to the terror of the valley's abundant peaceable wildlife.

The remainder of our journey passed uneventfully. We arrived at Tsumago at 4:48 PM, sunset exactly, and wound our way through the empty streets of the old post town. It felt as if we had stepped into a past era; the buildings were all simple and wooden, there were no cars, and the few street lamps that we passed flickered and sputtered like lanterns. Our stroll through the darkening streets brought us across the path of an elderly gentleman, who was picking up trash. He struck up a conversation.

He expressed a keen interest in where we had come from, as well as what had brought us to Tsumago that day. We explained that we had traveled from Ōzone that morning to hike the trail and see the autumn leaves. His eyes lit up at this—not, as it turned out, because he was appreciative of our interest in his town, but because he was intimately familiar with Ōzone's local karaoke parlor. As we were frequent patrons of the same establishment, we shared a few excited moments of mutual familiarity.

He inquired about our plans for the evening, as it was well and truly dark by that point. We explained that we hoped to enjoy a quick snack before taking a cab to our B&B in Nagiso, one town over. Our new friend intimated that he knew just the place for assistance on both fronts, then led us to one of the only shops in town that remained open.

It turned out to be a confectionery, which sold all manner of sugary snacks. It was owned by two middle-aged women, whose carefree laughter and effortless banter spoke of a bond that can only be found between sisters. They, too, expressed a great deal of interest in our plans for the night ahead. We shared them yet again and were met with what we judged to be an inordinate level of disbelief.

"No, no, no. That can't be right," the older sister insisted after we had informed them that we were staying at an Airbnb. "Only foreigners run Airbnb's, and there are no foreigners in the valley."

I, a foreigner in the valley, was quite taken aback by the matter-of-fact nature of her statement. Mildly offended, and growing concerned that I may have made a booking error, I showed them the location of our B&B. They feigned incredulity over this as well, at which point Fumika and I began to suspect that they were just having fun with the two grubby outsiders who had wandered into their shop at closing time.

Once the conversation reached a lull, the sisters offered to call us a cab. At this point, we realized that we hadn't seen a single car since arriving in Tsumago, let alone a cab, and that our phones were well outside of service range. Had we not crossed paths with the old man who led us to their shop, we may not have been able to order a taxi at all. Walking to our B&B would have taken over an hour along an unlit highway at night, so we were suddenly quite glad for the giggling sisters and their offhanded generosity. They even went so far as to brew us some tea while we waited outside their shop, so we bought some of their candied chestnuts in turn.

Thankfully, when our taxi arrived, the driver seemed more measured. He took one brief look at our B&B's location, let out an exaggerated *"Hai,"* and took off. He dropped us off at the convenience store next to our B&B ten minutes later, per our request.

To be clear, Fumika and I hadn't expected much from this B&B. We were still riding high from the majesty of Homma-san's villa scant weeks before, and the proprietor had made the somewhat dubious decision to list the lodging as a "Hut"—a descriptor that we found both worrisome and intriguing. Upon arriving, we were relieved to see that it met the basic requirements of a fully-fledged home, and a subsequent tour by the owner reassured us that it was not, in fact, a hovel.

Instead, it was a traditional wooden *kominka* of the sort that I had walked by countless times before but never had cause to enter. You see, many of the older Japanese towns have developed in such a way that houses and shops are interspersed randomly with no outwardly identifying characteristics. As a result, they tend to blend together into one long bank of indistinguishable wooden facades. Since Tsumago had already closed up prior to both of my visits, it had the appearance of a movie prop: a hastily-constructed series of buildings that looked like a real town from afar but would not hold up to much scrutiny.

Our B&B was in the nearby village of Nagiso, though, and proved to be a bona fide residence. Better still, it was charmingly rustic with a cozy attic and a small Zen garden. Once again, our paltry expectations for the quality of a B&B had proved misguided. Fumika and I spent a lovely night drinking tea beneath the stars in the zen garden before finally retiring to bed.

The next morning, we awoke to the sound of footsteps within the house. At one point in my life, this would have triggered within me a primal terror second only to "having my ankle grabbed from beneath the bed," but I had grown soft and trusting in Japan. I got out of bed with an unconcerned, "There must be some mistake," to Fumika, and went downstairs to confirm that there had, in fact, been some mistake. A cleaning crew had made a scheduling error and entered the house a few hours before our check-out.

They apologized and left, but the sudden knowledge that an indeterminate number of strangers could enter the home at will soured our interest in relaxing there any longer. We gathered our belongings, took one last deep breath in the Zen garden, and left to explore the surrounding area.

Now, I've spoken before about Seto, the town I taught in, and how every one of the 130,000 residents considered it a country backwater. And, by Japanese standards, they may have been correct. So believe me when I say that Nagiso, with a population barely exceeding 4,000, was painfully rural. The entire town was a rough assemblage of houses scattered, as if by shotgun, along the banks of the Kiso River, plus two shrines and a temple. By then, my fascination with all things Shinto had developed into an obsession, so I suggested we visit the closest of these. Fumika and I set off through the hilly streets.

Neither the first shrine nor the nearby temple had much to offer in the way of excitement, but they were refreshing nonetheless. From the latter, we walked past a small cemetery, following signs toward a hilltop park. As we should have guessed from the rather unkempt nature of the trail, which was littered with fallen trees and largely overgrown, the "park" proved to be little more than a collection of tree stumps arranged in a circle. Fumika and I brushed the leaves and moss off of what passed for a bench, then settled in to enjoy the rustle of leaves in the branches above. Much of the afternoon was spent in that manner, unconcerned that we would be disturbed. After all, it did not appear to be the sort of park that attracted many visitors.

When our seat grew uncomfortable, we made our way back down the briar-laden hillside. There was one last shrine to be seen within Nagiso, and we wanted to leave ample time for our return trip to Ōzone afterward.

We walked parallel to the river for some time before arriving at the shrine's supposed location. Met with only a golf course and a wrought-iron bridge, neither of which looked particularly venerable, we decided to search for the shrine along the banks of the river itself. We took a narrow path through some brambles toward the river.

The riverbed was (as we vaguely remembered remarking on the taxi ride into town the prior evening) littered with massive boulders. As Fumika and I searched for the shrine, we played a game of Climb the Biggest Rock—one of my childhood favorites. It took us farther and farther downstream, and farther still from the only entrance to the riverbed not covered in brambles. A short time later, we found and climbed what was indeed the Biggest Rock.

We sat there for a while, enjoying the sounds and sights of the river. Eventually, though, we grew a bit chilly, so we clambered down to continue our search for a safe path away from the riverbed. We identified a patch of brambles that promised only light pain, rather than excruciating agony, and pressed our way through and out...

Directly onto the threshold of Shiikawawaki Shrine. Although we had long since abandoned it as our destination, we couldn't have found it more perfectly if we'd tried.

The shrine was small, peaceful, and could thankfully be exited via a previously-unseen trail directly onto the golf course. We paid our quiet respects to the *kami* within, then continued onward toward the train station.

We did a few more things on our way to the station, such as walking across Nagiso's picturesque Momosuke Bridge. But, in truth, nothing occurred that would be of any particular interest to anyone but the two of us. All in all, I spent a laidback afternoon with my lovely girlfriend in the Japanese countryside before we returned, once more, to our daily lives.

# Epilogue

One month after that beautiful excursion into the unchartered depths of the Kiso River Valley, the year ended. Somehow, December had arrived unnoticed—first in days, then in weeks, then in great, leaping bounds that eclipsed the months in moments. At the end of the year, I said bittersweet farewells to the many people that I had come to know and love and, with a heavy heart, boarded a plane bound for home...

For a brief vacation, before promptly returning to Japan. Of course my initial plan to only stay for a year had undergone a million changes since I had arrived. How could it not, when I had?

When I left for Japan, I was an idealistic, well-meaning young man who had never truly left the bubble of his own reality. Under the immense pressure of restarting my life at the age of 24, however, I had grown so much as a person. And while there were certainly a few growing pains to start, by December I had begun to closely resemble a fully-functioning, self-sufficient adult.

So, what had I given up to purchase this year of nonstop enjoyment, cultural revelations, and personal growth?

Well, not much, actually. I was glad to see my family and friends again come New Years, but my home had remained, by and large, unchanged. Other people's lives had continued trucking along in my absence—time marches inexorably onward, whether or not you're there to take its measure—but that was to be expected. Had I chosen to end my Japanese adventure at the one-year mark, the entire experience would only have cost me a few small trips and milestones with my family. In their stead, I had gained a veritable lifetime's worth of experiences and personal development that I may never have found in America.

But, for me, my Japanese adventure had long since developed into something more permanent. I would be lying if I claimed my budding romance with Fumika had nothing to do with my decision to stay, but I had requested to extend my employment contract long before we had ever begun dating. When all was said and done, I simply wasn't *ready* to leave. For all of the breathtaking, remarkable things that I had seen and done, there was still so much that I had yet to discover.

So, at the beginning of January, almost to the day of my original departure, I returned to Japan. Since then, I have not regretted that decision once—although the COVID-19 pandemic has certainly made life more complicated. In my free time, I pursue my passions (i.e. writing this book), travel the country, and further explore Japanese culture. My first year in Japan was incredible; everything since has been even better.

Now that you've heard my story in all of its complicated, unfettered glory, it is my sincerest, most heartfelt desire that you will consider doing the same as I have done. Anyone reading this—regardless of race, sex, or financial situation—can make use of today's boundless connectivity to explore the world.

Time moves as imperceptibly as the tide. You never truly notice its passage until the tide has risen, and all that you had written in the sand is washed away. Whether it be for a month, a year, or a lifetime, I implore you: Before your tide has risen, go experience all that life has to offer.

## Stranger in a Homeland

Thank you so much for reading my book!

Your time and interest mean the world to me. I hope that you had fun and found something to take away into your own life.

If you enjoyed this book, I would really appreciate a review on Amazon.com. It only takes a moment, and is the best way for up-and-coming authors to gain exposure.

Let's chase the horizon together.

Made in the USA
Monee, IL
15 April 2021